POETIC LOGIC

The Role of Metaphor in Thought, Language, and Culture

by Marcel Danesi

Atwood Publishing
Madison, WI

POETIC LOGIC
THE ROLE OF METAPHOR IN THOUGHT, LANGUAGE, AND CULTURE
by Marcel Danesi

© 2004 Atwood Publishing, Madison, WI
www.atwoodpublishing.com

Cover design by Tamara Dever, TLC Graphics, www.tlcgraphics.com
Cover drawing by Carter Todd, *Going Back Home,* colored pencil, 2003.

Published with the cooperation of the Crossroads Center of the University of Toronto at Mississauga.

Vol. 1 in the Series: Language and Communication
Series Editors: Marcel Danesi and Linda J. Rogers

Library of Congress Cataloging-in-Publication Data

Danesi, Marcel, 1946-
  Poetic logic : the role of metaphor in thought, language, and culture / by Marcel Danesi.
      p. cm. — (Language and communication ; v. 1)
  Includes bibliographical references.
  ISBN 1-891859-49-8 (pbk.)
  1. Semantics (Philosophy) 2. Metaphor. 3. Psycholinguistics. 4. Metaphor—Psychological aspects. I. Title. II. Series.
  B840.D35 2004
  401'.43—dc22
                          2003027439

TABLE Of CONTENTS

PREFACE

The contemporary French semiotician and social critic Jean Baudrillard (1929–) made a comment a while back that stands, to this day, as truly insightful: "Everywhere one seeks to produce meaning, to make the world signify, to render it visible" (Baudrillard 1987, 7). *Homo sapiens* is indeed a "meaning-producing" species. In its quest to make the world signify, it has invented such things as language, art, music, mathematics, and science which, as Baudrillard aptly observes, make the world "visible," i.e., understandable in human terms. The faculty of the mind that guides our attempts to make sense of things was called *poetic logic* by the great Neapolitan philosopher Giambattista Vico (1688–1744) in his landmark treatise of 1725, *The New Science* (Bergin and Fisch 1984). Vico described poetic logic as a universal form of imaginative thinking that allows us to understand the world on our own terms. He maintained, however, that it is not possible to study poetic logic directly, since the mind cannot study itself! Nevertheless, he suggested that we could certainly gain a good understanding of what it reveals about human thinking by studying one of its most imaginative products—*metaphor*. As remarkable as that insight was, it is only today that metaphor has finally started to catch the attention of linguists and psychologists. However, the research on metaphor has yet to catch up to Vico, since it still lacks the notion of poetic logic to guide its mode of inquiry. One of the purposes for this book is, in fact, to present the case for poetic logic, for it would explain many (if not most) of the findings on metaphor that have been accumulating since at least the 1950s.

My fortuitous discovery of Vico in the 1970s is due to two late scholars, Robert J. Di Pietro of the University of Delaware and Giorgio Tagliacozzo, the founder of the Institute for Vico Studies in New York. I am forever grateful to them. My discovery has allowed me to carry out some of the most important and exciting research on language I have ever conducted in my professional career as a linguist and semiotician. One of the reasons for writing this book has been, in fact, to pass on some of that excitement to a broad audience. It is based on the notes I use to teach a course in anthropological linguistics at the University of Toronto. The classroom has forced me to rework the technical research findings on metaphor into an accessible form for broader consumption, extracting from them the main implications they have for studying language. I have thus written this book essentially as an introduction to *metaphorology*—as the field of metaphor study was called by the Italian semiotician and writer Umberto Eco (1976, 45) in the 1970s.

Metaphorical expressions are so common and pervasive in discourse that people hardly ever notice them. Although interest in metaphor is ancient, the scientific study of its relation to cognition and culture is a relatively recent phenomenon. And the interest has soared. Since about the mid-1950s the amount of linguistic and psychological research on metaphor has been mind-boggling. I myself have compiled over 5000 bibliographical entries on metaphor over the last few years. There is currently so much information on metaphor scattered in journals and books that it would take a gargantuan effort just to organize and classify it. My aim in this book is not to assemble the "facts on file," but rather to take a look at the larger picture through the Vichian lens of poetic logic. For this reason, I have had to be highly selective. I therefore warn the reader, from the outset, that the specific contents of each chapter reflect my own particular approach to metaphor and my own preferences. The knowledgeable reader will, thus, find various gaps, from missing authors to missing data and theoretical notions. In a single volume, it is simply impossible to be comprehensive and overarching. Nevertheless, I have attempted to cast as wide a net as possible within the confines of a general treatment. The perspective thus gained from reading this book will, I hope, be an exciting one for anyone interested in the nature of language. I should also mention that this is not a book on Vico, but rather a book on metaphor as seen in terms of Vico's most important discovery—poetic logic. Readers interested in current research on Vico can consult the articles published in either or both of the two journals devoted to making the philosopher's ideas known throughout the world—the *Bollettino del Centro di Studi Vichiani* (which publishes only in Italian) and *New Vico Studies* (which publishes in English). Both journals contain extensive bibliographies of publications on Vico and on the applications of Vichian ideas to the study of the arts, sciences, and humanities.

I would like to thank, above anyone else, my students at the University of Toronto. Their critical responses to my lectures, along with the many enthusiastic and meaningful discussions I have had with them over the years, have encouraged me to write this text for a broader audience. I must also thank Linda Babler, director of Atwood Publishing, for her support and encouragement. I truly hope not to disappoint either Linda or my students.

Marcel Danesi
University of Toronto, 2004

Chapter 1

METHAPHOR
& POETIC LOGIC

Midway between the unintelligible
and the commonplace, it is metaphor
which most produces knowledge.
— Aristotle (384–322 BC)

The types of questions that children ask are remarkable for their acumen. That acumen is manifest when, seemingly out of the blue, a child confronts us with a question such as "What is love?" The spontaneity and universality of such questions indicate that they are probably motivated by a need to understand the world that is evidently built into the human brain at birth.

Now, consider what kind of response we might give to the child's question. One answer that we certainly would not give is a "dictionary" definition of love—for the simple reason that the child would not understand it. What we are more likely to do is to relate the experience of love to something that is familiar to the child: e.g., "Love is the feeling you get when your mommy or daddy kisses you;" "Love is what you feel for your brother or sister when they have been away from home for a while;" and so on and so forth. If we are truly enterprising, we might even tell the child a story that illustrates what love is all about. We say and do things like this all the time because we intuitively know that children will grasp an abstract concept such as *love* only when it is exemplified concretely or in some narrative way. Concrete and narrative exemplifications are, by their very nature, *metaphorical* strategies. They are effective explanatory strategies because they allow us to make the world "visible," to quote Baudrillard one more time (preface).

Because we resort to metaphor so instinctively when we explain things to children, we hardly ever think of it as a trace to the workings of the human mind. Our tendency is, on the contrary, to consider it a mere "figure of speech"—a rhetorical strategy for making ideas more comprehensible or colorful. However, if the contemporary research findings on metaphor are even partially correct, then this view is an incorrect one. There is much more to metaphor than meets the eye (pardon my metaphor). As Giambattista Vico claimed two and a half centuries ago, it reveals how we make sense of certain things and, therefore, it is a trace to the "sense-making faculty" of the human mind, which he called *poetic logic* (preface). Discussing how this is so will be the goal of this book.

The Discovery of Metaphor

The discovery of metaphor is due to the Greek philosopher Aristotle (384–322 BC), who coined the term—itself as a metaphor (from Greek *meta* "beyond" and *pherein* "to carry") (Aristotle 1952a, 1457 ff.). Legend has it that the great philosopher thought up the term after one of his pupils posed the following question to him: "What is life?" As the (probably fictitious) story goes, Aristotle thought about the question for a moment and then answered: "Life is a stage." Enlightened by the master's response, the pupil thanked him and then purportedly went about with his normal business.

Even if the incident never occurred, the fact remains that Aristotle's answer was probably the only way for him to make the concept of life understandable to his pupil without embarking upon a long and cumbersome disquisition on it. As Aristotle knew, *life* is a concept which refers to something that we grasp intuitively, but which seems to defy a straightforward explanation or demonstration. Unlike visible things, such as animals, objects, and plants, life cannot be "shown" to someone directly. However, by comparing it to a *stage*, Aristotle did exactly that (in an imaginary sense). A stage is a platform upon which life can be shown to an audience through the roles of the characters on the stage, through the actions that unfold on it, and so on and so forth. Aristotle's metaphor reminded his pupil of that fact. But, in so doing, it actually revealed something much more profound. The very fact that Aristotle linked the two things in the first place indicates that, in his mind (and that of his pupil), life and stages were suggestive ontologically of each other.

The theater itself may, in fact, have come about in order to make life intelligible. With its characters and plots, it has always been perceived as an art form through which life can be examined. The theater remains, to this day, an overarching metaphor for life. In any of its modern versions (from cinema to television sitcoms), it continues to have great suasive power because it puts *life* on display in a concrete and understandable way. The ontological linkage between life and the stage is also the reason why we commonly use theater terms in conversations about life. For example, if we ask someone "What is your life like?" we are likely to get a response such as "My life is a comedy" or "My life is a farce," from which we can draw specific inferences:

Life Is a Stage

Theater Genre	Characteristics	Inferences
comedy	A dramatic work that is light and often humorous or satirical in tone and that usually contains a happy resolution of a ludicrous conflict.	If someone were to claim that his or her is a **comedy,** we would infer that the person perceives it as a sequence of ludicrous events.
tragedy	A drama or literary work in which the main character is brought to ruin or suffers extreme sorrow, especially as a consequence of a tragic flaw, a moral weakness, or an inability to cope with unfavorable circumstances.	If someone were to claim that his or her is a **tragedy,** we would infer that the person perceives it to unfold as a series of calamitous events that imbue his or her existence with sorrow; or else we could infer that the person is incapable of dealing with unfavorable circumstances.
farce	A light dramatic work in which highly improbable plot situations, exaggerated characters, and often slapstick elements are used for humorous effect.	If someone were to claim that his or her is a **farce,** we would infer that the person perceives it to be laughable because of the improbable events that characterize it.

Aristotle's metaphor, in fact, permeates all kinds of discourses as a template for understanding life in its many details, complexities, and vicissitudes. Psychologists, for instance, refer to the inclination to lie in order to emphasize the truth as the "Othello effect," in obvious reference to Shakespeare's character; people talk commonly of "promethean strength" in reference to the mythical personage of Greek theater, Prometheus; and the list could go on and on. Clearly, metaphor is hardly just a figure of speech, as is commonly believed. In actual fact, it reveals how we think, how we talk, and why certain things are the way they are. Incredibly, no special intellectual powers or advanced linguistic training are required to produce or understand metaphors. Every child is born with the faculty to do so. That faculty was called poetic logic by Vico.

Needless to say, Aristotle's metaphor is understandable only to someone who is familiar with stages. What if this were not the case? The power of poetic logic lies in the fact that it allows people to come up with a metaphorical expression to render the same concept intelligible. Indeed, *life* could be compared to virtually anything that would make sense in a specific cultural context, provided that it is exemplary of life in some way. So, for example, a statement such as *life is a river* coined in a culture where rivers play an important role in sustaining life would be "poetically logical" and, thus, highly effective in getting the job of explaining what life means done.

Aristotle saw metaphor as a product of proportional reasoning. For example, in the metaphor *Old age is the evening of life*, a proportion can be set up as follows: **A** = *old age*, **B** = *life*, **C** = *evening*, **D** = *day*; and, thus, **A** is to **B** as **C** is to **D**. The reasoning involved can be broken down as follows —the period of childhood is to life as the morning is to the day; the period of adulthood is to life as the afternoon is to the day; hence, old age is to life as the evening is to the day. This proportion, incidentally, pervades mythical and literary traditions throughout the world. It is found, for example, in the legend of the Sphinx—the mythical creature with the head and breasts of a woman, the body of a lion, a serpent tail, and the wings of a bird—who guarded entrance to the ancient city of Thebes. When Oedipus approached the city of Thebes, so the story goes, the gigantic Sphinx confronted him, posing the following riddle to him: "What is it that has four feet in the morning, two at noon, and three at night?" Failure to answer it correctly meant instant death—a fate that had befallen all who had ventured to Thebes before Oedipus. The fearless Oedipus answered: "Man, who crawls on all fours as a baby, then walks on two legs, and finally needs a cane in old age." Upon hearing the correct answer, the Sphinx killed itself, and Oedipus entered Thebes as a hero for having gotten rid of the terrible monster that had kept the city enslaved for a long period of time.

Various versions of the Sphinx's riddle exist. The one paraphrased above is from the play *Oedipus Rex* by the Greek dramatist Sophocles (c. 496–406 BC). Whatever its version, it is evidence that, since the dawn of history, people come to an understanding of life through metaphor. As humanity's first recorded puzzle, the Riddle of the Sphinx provides us, in fact, with an early model of how poetic logic manifests itself in human affairs.

The Neglect of Metaphor

Given the far-reaching implications of Aristotle's discovery, why is it that we still think of metaphor, by and large, as a simple figure of speech over two millennia later? Paradoxically, it may have been Aristotle himself who ingrained the strictly rhetorical view of metaphor in Western philosophical thinking by affirming that, as knowledge-productive as it was, the most common function of metaphor in human life was to spruce up more basic literal ways of speaking and thinking (Aristotle 1952a, 34). Aristotle's "literalist" view of meaning has remained a dominant one to this day in Western philosophical and linguistic traditions, with metaphor being either ignored or else condemned as a defect of human reasoning. The source of the latter view is, probably, John Locke's (1632–1704) characterization of metaphor as a "fault" in his *Essay Concerning Human Understanding* (Locke 1690, 34):

> If we would speak of things as they are, we must allow that all the art of rhetoric, besides order and clearness, all the artificial and figurative application of words eloquence hath invented, are for nothing else but to insinuate wrong ideas, move the passions, and thereby mislead the judgment; and so indeed are perfect cheats: and therefore, however laudable or allowable oratory may render them in harangues and popular addresses, they are certainly, in all discourses that pretend to inform or instruct, wholly to be avoided; and where truth and knowledge are concerned, cannot but be thought a great fault, either of language or person that makes use of them.

Thomas Hobbes (1588–1679) also inveighed fiercely against metaphor, characterizing it as an obstacle to communication, a source of ambiguity and obscurity, and thus, a feature of language to be eliminated from true philosophical and scientific discourse. Hobbes (1656) came to possess this view of metaphor because he believed that the laws of arithmetic mirrored the laws of human thought, and thus that the only meaningful form of philosophical discourse was of the same "literal" kind as the one used to explicate mathematical notions.

Another likely reason for the neglect of metaphor may be Aristotle's explanation of metaphor as a proportion (above)—an explanation that has come to be known as *comparison theory*. This in no way implies that it is an irrelevant theory. On the contrary, as Umberto Eco (1984, 88) has aptly pointed out, despite "the thousands and thousands of pages written about metaphor" since Aristotle formulated his theory, no single explanation has ever really eclipsed it. But the Aristotelian view does not explain the impulse to metaphorize in the first place (Di Pietro 1976). It is a rhetorical theory, not a psychological or philosophical one. The influential Roman rhetorician Quintilian (c. 35–100 AD) subsequently entrenched the rhetorical view even further by claiming that metaphor reveals nothing more than a decorative substitutive process. Thus, in an expression such as *Julius Caesar is a lion*, Quintilian claimed that we simply substitute the term *lion* for its literal counterpart, a *courageous man*, so as to make it more memorable or effective (Hausman 1989, 22–45; Way 1991, 27–60). But, like comparison theory, Quintilian's *substitution* explanation tells us nothing about the psychological motivation for the substitution in the first place.

Such views are based on the belief that literal meaning is the "default" form of semantic systems, whereby forms (words, phrases, sentences, etc.) encode referents in a straightforward one-to-one fashion. However, as I shall attempt to argue in this book, literalist theories are virtually useless for understanding semantic systems in their origins.

Giambattista Vico and Friedrich Nietzsche

In the medieval period, no less a philosopher than St. Thomas Aquinas (1225–1274) went contrary to the literalist grain by claiming, in his *Summa Theologica* (1266–1273), that the writers of Holy Scripture presented "spiritual truths" under the "likeness of material things" because that was the only way in which humans could grasp such truths, thus implying that metaphor was a tool of cognition, not just a feature of rhetorical flourish (quoted in Davis and Hersh 1986, 250):

> It is befitting Holy Scripture to put forward divine and spiritual truths by means of comparisons with material things. For God provides for everything according to the capacity of its nature. Now it is natural to man to attain to intellectual truths through sensible things, because all our knowledge originates from sense. Hence in Holy Scripture spiritual truths are fittingly taught under the likeness of material things.

But despite St. Thomas's discerning observation, philosophers continued largely to ignore metaphor. It was the Neapolitan philosopher Giambattista Vico (1688–1744) who attempted to spark interest in it over four centuries later, emphasizing that metaphor was indeed evidence of how "knowledge originates from sense," as St. Thomas had so aptly put it. Vico's characterization of our sense-making capacity as poetic logic is the first true psychological theory of metaphor. Incredibly, it has remained virtually unknown among psychologists and linguists. Discussing the reasons for this are beyond the objectives of the present discussion (see, for instance, Danesi 1995). Suffice it to say that the main reason is that, although the "rediscovery of Vico" in philosophy in the middle part of the twentieth century coincided chronologically with the "rediscovery of metaphor" in the human sciences, the two rediscoveries occurred on separate paths of the academic terrain. My goal here is to make these paths cross once and for all—a goal that has actually been pursued by a host of scholars since the 1950s, but with little impact on the mainstream (e.g., Pagliaro 1950; Apel 1975; Bonfante 1980; Di Cesare 1988, 1993, 1995; Pennisi 1988; Modica 1988; Battistini 1995; Leezenberg 1995).

Like Aristotle, Vico saw metaphor as a strategy for explicating or exemplifying an abstract notion such as *life*. However, he went much further in claiming that the strategy itself resulted from an association of sense between what is unknown and what is familiar: "It is another property of the human mind that whenever men can form no idea of distant and unknown things, they judge them by what is familiar and at hand" (Bergin and Fisch 1984, 122). The association, however, is not just a matter of convenience or expedience. Rather, the two parts of the metaphor suggest each other phenomenologically. In effect, by saying that *life is a stage* we are also implying that *stages are life*. The two parts are hardly combined through a mere act of comparison.

Vico's view of metaphor was largely ignored by his contemporaries. Mainstream philosophers of the era, and of the immediately succeeding one, such as G. W. F. Hegel (1770–1831) and John Stuart Mill (1806–1873), continued to insist that metaphor was no more than a decorative accessory to literal language. The exceptions to this mindset were Immanuel Kant (1724–1804), who mentioned in his *Critique of Pure Reason* (1781) that figurative language was evidence of how the mind attempted to understand unfamiliar things, and Friedrich Nietzsche (1844–1900), who came to see metaphor as humanity's greatest flaw, because of its subliminal power to persuade people into believing it on its own terms (Gumpel 1984, 25–28; Crawford 1988; Schrift 1990).

Nietzsche (1873) divided human thought into two domains—the domain of perception, consisting of impressions and sensations, and the domain of conception, consisting of the ideas that the mind makes from perception. But conception, Nietzsche asserted, is not a straightforward inferential process, but rather, the result of linking impressions together. This linkage is imprinted in the structure of metaphor which, subsequently, has the effect of distorting the true perception of things, creating belief because it prods the mind into perceiving a resemblance among disparate things by simply linking them together in linguistic form. Metaphor is thus the source of our superstitions and of our religious belief systems. To put it simply, Nietzsche saw metaphor as a linguistic self-fulfilling prophecy. As Schrift (1985, 389) puts it: "Insofar as language is a mere semiotic, a simplified, falsified, man-made sign-system, and insofar as all thinking is possible only in and through the means which language provides, the 'knowledge' and 'truth' which are derived from language are seen by Nietzsche to fail to do the job which they are thought to perform." For Nietzsche, therefore, any attempt to create a universal system of knowledge based on language would be a totally vacuous enterprise because it would be no more than the product of a "construction" process linked to the language that the knowledge-makers happened to speak.

I. A. Richards and the Gestalt Psychologists

Modern-day interest in metaphor as a trace to the nature of human cognition, rather than as a mere figure of speech, is not due to a reappraisal of Vico or Nietzsche, but rather to the pivotal work of the early experimental psychologists in the latter part of the nineteenth century. The founders of the new discipline—the German physicist Gustav Theodor Fechner (1801–1887) and the German physiologist Wilhelm Wundt (1832–1920)—were the first to conduct experiments on how people processed figurative language (Wundt 1901, Staehlin 1914). Karl Bühler (1908), for instance, collected some truly intriguing data on how subjects paraphrased and recalled proverbs. He found that the recall of a given proverb was excellent if it was linked to a second proverb; otherwise the proverb was easily forgotten. Bühler concluded that metaphorical-associative thinking produced an effective retrieval form of memory and was, therefore, something to be investigated further by the fledgling science.

Shortly after Bühler's fascinating work, a movement within psychology, called the *Gestalt* movement, emerged to make the study of metaphor a primary target of research (Wertheimer 1923). Like Vico, the Gestalt psychologists saw metaphor as evidence of how we form abstractions from sensory perceptions (Osgood and Suci 1953; Brown, Leiter, and Hildum 1957; Asch 1958; Werner and Kaplan 1963; Koen 1965). Solomon Asch (1950), for instance, examined metaphors of sensation (*hot, cold, heavy,* etc.) in several unrelated languages as descriptors of emotional states. He found that *hot* stood for *rage* in Hebrew, *enthusiasm* in Chinese, *sexual arousal* in Thai, and *energy* in Hausa (a language spoken in northern Nigeria, Niger, and adjacent areas). This suggested to him that, while the specific emotion implicated varied from language to language, the metaphorical process did not. Simply put, people seemed to think of emotions in terms of physical sensations and expressed them as such. As Brown (1958a, 146) commented shortly after the publication of Asch's findings, there is "an undoubted kinship of meanings" in different languages that "seem to involve activity and emotional arousal;" and that this "kinship" is revealed through metaphor.

But the scholar who most kindled a broad scientific interest in metaphor was, in actual fact, not a psychologist, but a literary theorist. In his groundbreaking 1936 book, *The Philosophy of Rhetoric*, I. A. Richards (1893–1979) started a veritable revolution in thinking about metaphor by arguing persuasively that it hardly could be classified as a replacement of literal meaning for communicative or stylistic purposes, but rather that it produced a new psychologically powerful meaning that could never be encompassed by a simple literal paraphrase. In order to discuss how such meaning arose, Richards labeled the parts of the metaphor as follows: (1) he called the metaphorical concept itself the *tenor* (e.g., *life*); (2) he called the concrete notion to which it was linked the *vehicle* (e.g., a *stage*); and (3) he called the meaning produced by the linkage of the topic and vehicle the *ground (life is a stage = stages represent life)*. The tenor is now called *topic* in the relevant literature. Richards then claimed that the linkage was hardly a matter of mere comparison or substitution, but rather an entailment based on perception of relationship. Calling it the *ground*, Richards wanted clearly to imply that the topic and vehicle stood in relation to each other as do the figures in a painting. In strict psychological terms, the meaning inherent in *life is a stage* is perceived as a categorical "interaction" between *life* and *stages*. To put it more specifically, there is more to *life* than *stages*, and *stages* may have functions other than to represent *life*. But these two categories of human reality overlap considerably. If we represent each part of the metaphor with a circle, then the ground (meaning) is the area of intersection or overlap of the two circles:

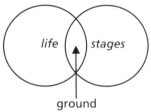

As a case-in-point of how Richard's *interactionist* view would explain the origination of a common metaphor, consider *John is a gorilla*. The topic in this case is a person named *John* and the vehicle the animal known as a *gorilla*. Portraying *John* as a *gorilla* implies that the two are alike in some way. The linkage generates an image of a person with gorilla-like characteristics and, vice versa, of a gorilla with human-like qualities. One image blends into the other in the same way that figures blend into each other in optical illusions. But this blending would not occur if the topic and vehicle were not perceived as exemplars of each other in the first place. This suggests a different, more general, level in metaphorization—one in which animals are perceived as exemplars of human personality and humans as types of animal. Changing the vehicle brings this out clearly. If one were to label *John* as a *snake*, a *pig*, or a *puppy*, rather than a *gorilla*, then our image of *John* would change in kind with each new vehicle—he would become serpentine, swine-like, and puppy-like in our imagination. Like Franz Kafka's (1883–1924) horrifying short story *Metamorphosis*, where the main character awakes one morning from a troubled dream to find himself changed in his bed to some kind of monstrous vermin, our perception of people (and of ourselves for that matter)

is altered (probably permanently) the instant we paint a metaphorical picture of their personalities in animal terms. The reason for this is that we perceive ourselves deep inside to be animals. Talking about people as if they were animals is a manifestation of this unconscious perception.

In *John is a gorilla*, the topic and vehicle are stated explicitly. But, as Perrine (1971) argued several decades after Richard's groundbreaking work, this is not always the case in metaphorization. In many metaphorical constructions, one or both of the separate parts can be implied. As can be seen below, the more the level of implicitness, the greater the psychological force of the metaphor (from Hoffman and Honeck 1980, 5):

Metaphor	Topic	Vehicle	Ground
The author's writings are useful groceries.	author's writings (explicit)	useful groceries (explicit)	The writings contain important ideas.
The optimist has congenital anesthesia.	optimist's attitude (explicit)	congenital amnesia (explicit)	The optimist is ignorant or unaware.
The chairman plowed through the discussion.	chairman (explicit-implicit)	plowing (explicit)	Committee work is hard.
He flung himself on his horse and rode madly off in all directions.	manner of riding (implicit)	madly in all directions (explicit)	He was in a mental state of excited confusion.
The furious phenomenon of five o'clock is overwhelming.	rush hour (implicit)	furious phenomenon of five o'clock (explicit)	Traffic is overwhelming and infuriating.
Great weights hang on small wires.	outcomes (implicit)	minor details (implicit)	Important events can depend on less important ones.

Like miniature poems, metaphors obviously stimulate our imagination, impelling us to glean sense from the interaction of their two parts. This "sense-producing" power of metaphor is the reason why we use it to make commentaries on all aspects of human life, and it is thus the reason why it informs the folk wisdom of a culture. The fable, for instance, is usually a tale about metaphorical animals, which are portraits of human personalities. The tale may also be about metaphorical trees, winds, streams, stones, and other natural objects. In effect, fables bring out our tendency to "animating the inanimate realm," and to "humanize the animal realm" as a means to understand both realms.

The philosopher Max Black (1962) formalized interactionist theory as follows. In the metaphor *John is a gorilla*, *John* is really an exemplar of the more general category of *people* and *gorilla* of the category of *simians*. The two categories are linked to each other because they are perceived to be subcategories of *animals:*

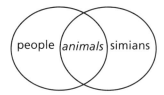

Black argued that this kind of linkage not only underlies common conceptualizations, but is also the creative backbone of science. A scientific theory is, in effect, a metaphorical inference. It is an example of what the great American semiotician, Charles Peirce (1839–1914), referred to as an *abduction* or "informed hunch." A classic example is the original theory of atomic structure formulated by the English physicist Ernest Rutherford (1871–1937). Rutherford never saw the inside of an atom with his eyes (nor has anyone else for that matter). So, he used his inner eye to produce a hunch that the atom has the same kind of structure that the solar system has, with electrons behaving like little planets orbiting around an atomic nucleus. Rutherford's model of atomic structure as a miniature solar system continues to make sense because we feel that the cosmos is structurally the same at all levels, from the microcosmic (the atomic) to the macrocosmic (the universe). As Black pointed out, this is so because we perceive the atom and the solar system to be subcategories of the same general category:

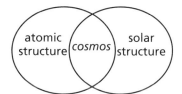

Conceptual Metaphor Theory

The pivotal work of Richards, Black, and the Gestalt psychologists did not penetrate mainstream psychology and linguistics in the 1960s and 1970s (e.g., Bickerton 1969; Grice 1975; Sperber and Wilson 1986; Fogelin 1988). The main reason for this was, arguably, the influence that the renowned American linguist Noam Chomsky (1928–) had on both disciplines. Chomsky went so far as to characterize metaphor as a "deviation" from fundamental linguistic rules (e.g., Chomsky 1964), and thus as something that should be ignored in the quest to understand the language faculty. It was only in the last two decades of the twentieth century that the Chomskyan paradigm came to be questioned by a growing number of linguists and psychologists, bringing about a true paradigm shift in the study of language.

The turning point was a 1977 study which showed that metaphor pervades common speech. Titled *Psychology and the Poetics of Growth: Figurative Language in Psychology, Psychotherapy, and Education*, the study —conducted by a team of psychologists headed by Howard Pollio— found that speakers of English uttered, on average, an astounding 3,000 novel metaphors and 7,000 idioms per week (Pollio, Barlow, Fine, and Pollio 1977). In other words, the study made it obvious to one and all that metaphor could hardly be construed as a deviation from linguistic rules, or a mere stylistic option to literal language. The study turned the tide in linguistics and psychology dramatically. Since then, the number of volumes, symposia, courses, articles, websites, and journals dealing directly with, or involving related work on, metaphor has become astronomical. The fact that I cannot possibly give even a schematic overview here of the relevant literature—for that would take several huge tomes —attests to how intense the interest in metaphor has become. Two years after the Pollio et al. study, the literary critic Booth (1979, 49) quipped that metaphor was "taking over not only the world of humanists but the world of the social and natural sciences as well." Booth went on to add facetiously that, if one were to count the number of bibliographical entries on metaphor published in the year 1977 alone, one would be forced to surmise that by the year 2039 there would be "more students of metaphor on Earth than people." In 1985 Noppen compiled a bibliography of post-1970 publications, which he updated in 1990 with Hols (Noppen and Hols 1990), showing how extensive the study of metaphor had become in such a short time. In 1986 metaphor even got its own journal, *Metaphor and Symbolic Activity*, which grew out of the *Metaphor Research Newsletter* published by R. R. Hoffman and M. K. Smith at Adelphi University (1982–1985). It is still being published, as I write, under the revised title *Metaphor and Symbol*, by Lawrence Erlbaum and Associates.

The 1979 collection of studies by Andrew Ortony, *Metaphor and Thought*, the 1980 anthology put together by R. P. Honeck and R. R. Hoffman, *Cognition and Figurative Language*, and the highly popular 1980 book by George Lakoff and Mark Johnson, *Metaphors We Live By*, set the groundwork for a new approach to the study of language that has since come to be known as *Conceptual Metaphor Theory* (CMT). The central notion on which CMT is implanted is that metaphorical meaning pervades language and thought. The literalist approach in linguistics asserts that we encode and decode linguistic messages on the basis of a literal meaning, deciding on a metaphorical one only when a literal interpretation is not possible (Grice 1975). But CMT has brought forward an enormous amount of evidence to show why this view is no longer tenable. If contextual information is missing from an utterance such as *The murderer is an animal*, our inclination is to interpret it metaphorically, not literally.

It is only if we are told that the *murderer* is an actual "animal" (a bear, a cougar, etc.) that a literal interpretation comes into focus.

Another critical finding of CMT research concerns so-called *nonsense* or *anomalous strings*. It was Noam Chomsky (1957) who first used such strings—e.g., *Colorless green ideas sleep furiously*—to argue that the syntactic rules of a language were independent from the semantic rules. Such strings have the "feel" of real sentences because they consist of real English words put together in a syntactically-appropriate fashion. This forces us to interpret the string as a legitimate, but meaningless, sentence —a fact which suggests that we process meaning separately from syntax. Of course, what Chomsky ignored is that although we do not extract literal meaning from such strings, we are certainly inclined to extract a metaphorical meaning from them. When people are asked to interpret them, they invariably came up with metaphorical meanings for them (Pollio and Burns 1977; Pollio and Smith 1979; Connor and Kogan 1980). This finding suggests, therefore, that we are inclined, by default, to glean metaphorical meaning from any well-formed string of words, and that literal meaning is probably the exception in the processing of strings. As Winner (1982, 253) has aptly put it, if "people were limited to strictly literal language, communication would be severely curtailed, if not terminated."

A third important finding of CMT is that metaphor implies mental imagery. In 1975, for instance, Billow found that a metaphor such as *The branch of the tree was her pony* invariably was pictured by his child subjects in terms of a girl riding a tree branch. Since the use of picture prompts did not significantly improve the imaging process or the time required to interpret metaphors, Billow concluded that metaphors were already high in imagery-content and, consequently, needed no prompts to enhance their interpretation. Incidentally, visually-impaired people have the same kind of imagery-content as do visually unimpaired people. The fascinating work of Kennedy (1984, 1993; Kennedy and Domander 1986) has shown that even congenitally blind people are capable of making appropriate line drawings of metaphorical concepts if they are given suitable contexts and prompts.

The publication that made CMT accessible and attractive to a large audience of linguists and psychologists was George Lakoff and Mark Johnson's 1980 book, *Metaphors We Live By*. The Lakoff-Johnson approach will be taken up in greater detail in the next chapter. For the present purpose, it is sufficient to provide some general comments on it. First, Lakoff and Johnson assert what Aristotle claimed two millennia before, namely, that there are two types of concepts—*concrete* and *abstract*. But the two scholars added a remarkable twist to the Aristotelian dichotomy. For Lakoff and Johnson, abstract concepts should not be viewed as being autonomous from concrete ones, but rather as "thought formulas" built up systematically from concrete associations. They thus renamed an abstract concept a *conceptual metaphor*. To grasp what this designates, recall the example above of *John* and the animals to which he was linked metaphorically (*gorilla, snake, pig, puppy*). When looked at globally, it is obvious that each specific metaphorical association *(John is a gorilla, John is a snake,* etc.) is an instantiation of a more general concept, which can be formalized with the formula: *people are animals*. This formula is an example of what Lakoff and Johnson call a conceptual metaphor:

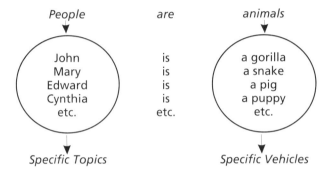

The two scholars then labeled each of the two parts of a conceptual metaphor *domains*—they called the *people* part the *target domain* because it is the abstract "target" of the conceptual metaphor; and they termed the *animals* part of the metaphor the *source domain* because it constitutes the class of vehicles that delivers the metaphor (the "source" of the metaphorical concept). The gist of Lakoff and Johnson's argument is that the metaphors people use commonly in everyday conversations are hardly disconnected flights of linguistic fancy, but rather instantiations of metaphorical thought formulas (conceptual metaphors) that crystallize systematically in speech. Specific metaphors (e.g., *John is a gorilla, Mary is a puppy,* etc.) are, in effect, traces to these formulas (e.g., *people are animals*). As mentioned briefly above, and as will be elaborated in subsequent chapters, the reason for correlating two domains is the *de facto* perception the two—humans and animals in this case—are interconnected in some psychological way. Indeed, as we shall see in the final chapter, metaphor is the strongest evidence that exists for supporting an *interconnectedness principle*, or the view that the human mind is programmed to perceive the things of the world as connected to each other in various ways, and that language is a trace to that perception.

As a practical example of how this principle guides our choice of words, let us assume hypothetically that I am not feeling well and that it is raining. I look at the rain dripping down my window. That sight will probably impel me to associate the droplets of rain to my emotional state. Now, it is this association that will tend to manifest itself in any discourse I will produce for some specific reason. For example, if someone were to ask me how I felt at that moment, I might say something such as *I'm feeling drippy today*. The choice of the word *drippy* is a trace to both my mood and the outside weather, given the context in which it was uttered. As it turns out, the expression I used is an instantiation of a conceptual metaphor—*mood is a meteorological state*. The same thought formula is the source of expressions such as *I'm under the weather today, The skies are shining on their lives*, and so on. We do not recognize the presence of such thought formulas in our speech because, over time, they have become automatic and effortless.

CMT has radically altered the ways in which semantic systems are studied today by a large number of psychologists and linguists. As discussed above, since ancient times metaphor has been studied as a rhetorical device, rather than as a trace to human thought. In rhetorical tradition, metaphor is still viewed as one of various tropes. Below are the main ones:

- *Climax* is the arrangement of words, clauses, or sentences in the order of their importance, the least forcible coming first and the others rising in potency: *It is an outrage to scoff at her; it is a crime to ridicule her; but to deny her freedom of speech, what shall I say of this?*

- *Anticlimax* is the opposite trope, whereby ideas are sequenced so that they abruptly diminish in importance, generally for satirical effect: *I will shoot him down first, and then I will talk to him.*

- *Antithesis* refers to the juxtaposition of two words, phrases, clauses, or sentences contrasted or opposed in meaning in such a way as to give emphasis to contrasting ideas: *To err is human, to forgive divine.*

- *Apostrophe* is the technique by which an actor turns from the audience, or a writer from readers, to address a person who usually is either absent or deceased, or else to address an inanimate object or an abstract idea: *Hail, Freedom, whose visage is never far from sight.*

- *Euphemism* is the substitution of a delicate or inoffensive term or phrase for one that has coarse, sordid, or other unpleasant connotations, as in the use of *lavatory* or *rest room* for *toilet*.

- *Exclamation* is a sudden outcry expressing strong emotion: *Oh vile, vile, person!*

- *Hyperbole* is the use of exaggeration for effect: *My friend drinks oceans of water.*
- *Litotes* is the technique of understatement so as to enhance the effect of the ideas expressed: *Carl Jung showed no inconsiderable analytical powers as a psychologist.*
- *Simile* is the technique of specific comparison by means of the words *like* or *as* between two kinds of things: *You're as light as a feather.*
- *Metonymy* is the use of a word or phrase for another to which it bears an important relation, as the effect for the cause, the abstract for the concrete, etc.: *She's the head of our family.*
- *Conceit* is an elaborate, often extravagant metaphor or simile, for making an analogy between totally dissimilar things: *Love is a worm.*
- *Irony* refers to a dryly humorous or lightly sarcastic mode of speech, in which words are used to convey a meaning contrary to their literal sense: *I really love the pain you give me.*
- *Onomatopoeia* is the imitation of natural sounds: *the humming bee, the cackling hen,* etc.
- *Oxymoron* is the combination of two seemingly contradictory or incongruous words: *My life is a living death.*
- *Paradox* is a statement that appears contradictory or inconsistent: *She's a well-known secret agent.*
- *Personification* is the representation of inanimate objects or abstract ideas as living beings: *Necessity is the mother of invention.*
- *Rhetorical Question* is a questioning strategy that is intended not to seek information but to assert more emphatically the obvious answer to what is asked: *You do understand what I mean, don't you?*
- *Synecdoche* is the technique whereby the part is made to stand for the whole, the whole for a part, the species for the genus, etc.: *The President's administration contained the best brains in the country.*

This typology has been completely revamped within CMT. The trend within it is to consider some of above tropes as manifestations of metaphorical reasoning, rather than as separate tropes. Thus, for example, personification (*My cat speaks Italian, Mystery resides here*, etc.) is now viewed as a specific kind of conceptual metaphor, in which *people* is the source domain: e.g., *animals are people, ideas are people*, etc. Some of the above categories—onomatopoeia, metonymy, synecdoche, and irony—continue to be viewed as separate tropes and thus treated separately.

The work in CMT has shown, in sum, that many, if not most, of our abstract ideas are metaphorical in structure. No wonder, then, that interest in metaphor has become widespread in many disciplines. But even so, by and large people still think of metaphor as a stylistic device of language, used by poets and writers to decorate or make their messages more effective or ornate. But nothing could be further from the truth. Lakoff and Johnson (1980, 3) put it as follows:

> Metaphor is typically viewed as characteristic of language alone, a matter of words rather than thought and action...On the contrary, metaphor is pervasive in everyday life, not just in language but in thought and action.

There are a few caveats that must be made from the outset vis-à-vis CMT. First, whether or not all abstract concepts are structured metaphorically is a question that is open to research and debate. Second, even if this were so, it must not be forgotten that there are aspects of language that are not metaphorical. But despite these cautions, the current research on the comprehension and production of metaphor within CMT has made it no longer tenable to assign figurative meaning to some subordinate category vis-à-vis literal meaning. In fact, metaphor is so common in discourse and cultural representation that we hardly ever realize how it influences our perceptions and beliefs (as Nietzsche warned). In a compelling 1978 book, *Illness as Metaphor*, the writer Susan Sontag argued that, although illnesses are not metaphors, people are invariably predisposed to think of specific illnesses in metaphorical ways. Using the example of cancer, Sontag pointed out that in the not-too-distant past the very word *cancer* was said to have killed some patients who would not have necessarily succumbed to the malignancy from which they suffered: "As long as a particular disease is treated as an evil, invincible predator, not just a disease, most people with cancer will indeed be demoralized by learning what disease they have" (Sontag 1978, 7). Sontag's point that people suffer more from conceptualizing metaphorically about their disease than from the disease itself is, indeed, a well-taken and instructive one.

Poetic Logic

The modern-day rediscovery of metaphor brings us back full circle to Vico. While much has been documented within CMT on the role of metaphor in language and thought, there is nothing in CMT that was not prefigured by Vico in his *New Science*. Moreover, CMT would be greatly enhanced as a theoretical enterprise if it were to seriously consider and adopt Vico's notion of poetic logic. We are all born poets, Vico suggested, using our senses to link things together into holistic ideas. It is this "linking through sense" capacity that makes the human mind so unique and powerful. Metaphor, which Vico defined as a "fable in brief," is a trace to this capacity:

> All the first tropes are corollaries of this poetic logic. The most luminous and therefore the most necessary and frequent is metaphor. It is most praised when it gives sense and passion to insensate things, in accordance with the metaphysics above discussed, by which the first poets attributed to bodies the being of animate substances, with capacities measured by their own, namely sense and passion, and in this way made fables of them. Thus every metaphor so formed is a fable in brief (Bergin and Fisch 1984, 404).

The notion of poetic logic is singular in the histories of philosophy and psychology. Vico articulated it in an era when what can be called *computationism* was beginning to take hold of philosophy (Danesi 1995). This is the belief that the human mind is a kind of machine programmed by Nature to receive and produce information in mathematically-determinable ways. In Vico's times, German mathematician and philosopher Gottfried Leibniz (1646–1716) had already built one of the first devices that could perform elementary arithmetical operations by means of interconnected rotating cylinders which, Leibniz maintained, modeled human thought processes in their essence (Churchland 1988, 99). As mentioned above, at mid-century Thomas Hobbes defined human thinking bluntly as arithmetical computation: i.e., as a process akin to the addition and subtraction of numbers (Hobbes 1656). The idea that mathematical laws mirrored mental processes and that, in principle, computing machines capable of thought could be built had entered the domain of philosophy. At about the same time, French mathematician and philosopher René Descartes (1596–1650) elaborated the view that the mind's activities were essentially algorithmic in nature and that they were independent of the body (Descartes 1637). A century later, British philosopher David Hume (1711–1776) put forward the notion that the mind could itself be studied by the laws of physics (Hume 1749).

The nineteenth century witnessed a further spread and refinement of computationism as a result of great advances in the theory of formal logic. The British mathematician George Boole (1815–1864) was the one who designed the first true system of formal logic which, he claimed, represented the main laws of thought (Boole 1854). German mathematician Gottlob Frege (1848–1925) expanded the Boolean paradigm, completing the edifice of modern formal logic (Frege 1879). Frege's work greatly influenced British philosopher Bertrand Russell (1872–1970) who, together with his compatriot Alfred North Whitehead (1861–

1947), synthesized the Boolean-Fregean system into a series of propositions that gave formal logic an overarching structure (Russell and Whitehead 1913). Their work led directly in the 1930s and 1940s to the first serious attempts to take the study of mind "out of the body," so as to be able to study it more objectively in the form of mathematical rules that were claimed to mirror the brain's thought processes. This led to the founding of artificial intelligence as a science designed to model human intelligence in computer programs. The ground-breaking work of the British mathematician Alan Turing (1912–1954), of the American engineer Claude Shannon (1916–2001), of the American computer scientist Norbert Wiener (1894–1964), and of the Hungarian-born American mathematician John von Neumann (1903–1957) provided the theoretical concepts for representing information independently of its specific content and of the devices that carried it. Turing's (1936, 1963) work on finite-state automata showed that the simple architecture of a four-operation machine—*move right, move left, write a slash, erase a slash*—could in principle carry out any recursive function. As we shall see in chapter 3, recursion is considered to be the basis of language creativity by some linguists. Turing's machine is still thought by many to be a physical model of human thinking. Claude Shannon (1948; Shannon and Weaver 1949) demonstrated that information of any kind could be described in terms of binary choices between equally probable alternatives. Wiener (1949) refined this idea further, showing it to characterize machine and human information-processing. And von Neumann (1958) built a rudimentary computer that allowed him to point out the remarkable similarities between mechanical and neural systems.

By the late 1950s, enthusiasm was growing over the possibility that artificial intelligence systems could be designed to carry out human thinking, and that the brain could finally be studied as an information-processing device. During the subsequent decade, advances in computer technology fuelled the excitement further. Computer terms to refer to mental processes, such as *storage, retrieval,* and *processing*, started to proliferate, shaping the technical lexicon and discourse of psychology and philosophy (MacCormac 1976; Hoffman 1980; Gentner 1982; Sternberg 1990). By the 1990s, extremist forms of computationism emerged, portraying human beings as no more than protoplasmic robots. The following citation from Konner (1991, 120) is a case-in-point:

> What religious people think of as the soul or spirit can perhaps be fairly said to consist of just this: the intelligence of an advanced machine in the mortal brain and body of an animal. And what we call culture is a collective way of using that intelligence to express and modify the emotions of that brain, the impulse and pain and exhilaration of that body.

The view that the mind and computers are similar in structure and function, both mirroring the same kinds of mathematical features is a fruitless one because it misses the point of how mathematical ideas come into being in the first place, as I have argued elsewhere (Danesi 2002). Mathematical ideas are not ingrained in the mind. They must first be imagined. It is only after they have been discovered through the power of the imagination, that they can be organized by the rational part of the mind into principles and systems of computation. Computers can easily simulate these because they exist as already-made inventions. They cannot call new principles into existence. In a word, computers are devoid of poetic logic. And because of this, the view of the mind as a complex computation device is simply useless, producing cumbersome theories that reveal nothing more than the complexity of their congeners. As Barrett (1986, 47) has phrased it, the "pseudo-precise language" of computationists "leaves us more confused about the matters of ordinary life than we would otherwise be."

To grasp how mathematical discoveries come about through the power of poetic logic, consider the discovery of *series*. In mathematics, a series is a sequence of numbers, called *terms*, that are generated by some rule. For example, the sequence of numbers {1, 3, 5, 7, 9,...} is a series because each term in it differs from the preceding one by 2. Although the concept itself was known even in antiquity, history suggests that the systematic investigation of series started after a remarkable discovery by the great German mathematician Karl Friedrich Gauss (1777–1855). The story goes that Gauss was only ten years old when he purportedly dazzled his math teacher with his exceptional mathematical abilities. One day, the teacher asked the class to cast the sum of all the numbers from one to one hundred: $1 + 2 + 3 + 4 + \ldots + 100 = ?$ Gauss raised his hand within seconds, giving the correct response of 5,050. When his teacher asked little Karl how he was able to come up with the answer so quickly, he is said to have replied (more or less) as follows:

> There are 49 pairs of numbers between one and one hundred that add up to one hundred: $1 + 99 = 100, 2 + 98 = 100, 3 + 97 = 100$, and so on. That makes 4,900, of course. The number 50, being in the middle, stands alone, as does 100, being at the end. Adding 50 and 100 to 4,900 gives 5,050.

In effect, Gauss had discovered and proven how to sum an arithmetical series: {1, 2, 3, ... 100}. Without going here into details, it is sufficient to note that Gauss's brilliant insight was not due to any feature of computational thinking. It was a product of poetic logic, whereby he saw a pattern that no one else had seen and, then, was able to make something of his insight. Computers may also stumble across patterns, but would have no idea what to do with them once they have! Anecdotes such as this one abound in the history of mathematics. They reveal that mathematics is the end result of a search for pattern and the creation of linkages among ideas. It is only after the patterns and linkages have been unraveled that they are organized into principles and systems of computation. Mathematics does indeed mirror the human mind, but clearly not in the way that computationists claim that it does.

The computer is a marvelous "note pad," as Kosslyn (1983, 116) characterizes it. But it is hardly a model of the poetic part of the human mind—the part which led Gauss to see a pattern that no one else had seen before. Poetic logic guides all discovery and invention. It has liberated human beings from the constraints imposed on all other organisms by biology and on machines by the laws of mechanics and electronics. As Verene (1981, 101) observes, it allows humans "to know from the inside" by extending "what is made to appear from sensation beyond the unit of its appearance and to have it enter into connection with all else that is made by the mind from sensation." Mathematics is one of humanity's greatest achievements. Human beings did not inherit mathematics from their biological legacy. They created it through the power of poetic logic to discover and understand pattern as it manifests itself in Nature and human affairs.

The debate on the nature of mind goes back to antiquity. Plato (427?–347? BC), for instance, saw ideas as separate from the biology of the senses. The circle, he claimed, is something that is born totally within the confines of the mind, given that it can be found nowhere in Nature as such. Thus, since the concept of the circle cannot be induced from sensory observation, then it must be innate. Descartes (1637) reinforced Plato's theory of innate ideas, claiming that the mind was separate from the body. Vico challenged the Platonic-Cartesian view because it told us nothing about how we invent such things as circles. Mathematical figures, names, and all the other concepts that make up the meaning substance of human cultures are the result of insight, inference, and linkage. The ancient names of the gods, for instance, were humanity's first metaphorical models for explaining phenomenological events. *Jove* was a metaphor for the thundering sky. Once the sky was called *Jove*, all other experiences of the same phenomenon could be "found again" in the name. *Jove* is a conscious metaphorical separation of the sky from the earth, of the divine from the human world. From these metaphorical ideas, the first conscious humans learned to make sense together. The ideas thus formed the basis for the creation of the first human institutions.

Poetic logic is evidence that we use our imagination in tandem with our senses to understand the world. Poets, artists, and mathematicians have always known this and expressed it in their works. For example, in the Middle Ages, the great Italian poet Dante (1265–1321) showed the world how the poetic understanding of things was intertwined with the human spirit and the flux of history. In his masterpiece, the *Divine Comedy*, which he began around 1307 and completed shortly before his death, Dante took his readers on a poetic journey through hell, purgatory, and heaven. In each of these three realms Dante met with mythological, historical, and contemporary personages. Each was a metaphorical personification of a particular human fault or virtue, either religious or political.

But poets are not the only ones who use metaphor. Everyone—from common folk to artists, musicians, and scientists—utilizes it on a routine basis to make sense of the world, to render it "visible," as Baudrillard so aptly put it (preface). However, attempting to understand the source of metaphor—poetic logic—constitutes a problem in circularity, since it cannot be studied without the investigator using his or her own poetic logic. Its workings can, nevertheless, be observed in metaphor itself, as Vico argued. For this reason, my focus in the remaining chapters of this book will be on the findings coming out of the field of CMT, for these provide the kinds of insights that might finally allow us to get a firm scientific understanding of this truly remarkable human faculty of mind, albeit an indirect one.

Chapter 2

THOUGHT

All thought must, directly or indirectly,
by way of certain characters, relate
ultimately to intuitions, and therefore,
with us, to sensibility, because in no other
way can an object be given to us.
— Immanuel Kant (1724–1804)

What is thought? How does one go about investigating it, since it cannot be separated from the thought of the investigator? These questions have always plagued philosophers. It can be argued, in fact, that philosophy's inability to come up with satisfactory answers to them is what led to the foundation of scientific psychology in the latter part of the nineteenth century—an enterprise whose objective was, and continues to be, to study human thought by observing its manifestations in subjects as they perform various experimental tasks. But psychology, too, has hardly provided satisfactory answers to the fundamental questions of philosophy, despite its clever experimental approach. As we saw in the previous chapter, in the middle part of the twentieth century, a new approach emerged, called *artificial intelligence* (AI), which put forward the intriguing possibility of taking thought "out of the brain," so to speak, so as to be able to study it objectively outside of the brain in the form of computer programs designed to simulate human thinking. AI has since become a flourishing science, leading to the development of computer systems that can diagnose diseases and locate minerals in the earth, among many other things. But, one may ask, does computer simulation truly provide insight into human thought? Computer programs can only follow a strict set of instructions, made by human programmers. As such, therefore, they put on display the ingenuity of their designers, but tell us nothing about how the designers went about designing the programs in the first place.

AI is really no more than a sophisticated modern version of computationism (chapter 1). It thus comes as little surprise to find that, when it comes to metaphor, AI researchers either skirt around the relevant research findings by simply ignoring them, or else dismiss metaphor outright as an irrelevant deviation from those basic thought processes. Thus, despite its achievements, AI has not solved the problem of finding a suitable way to study human thought. Apparently, it is either ignorant of, or disinterested in, the insight of Giambattista Vico over two and a half centuries ago that access to the human mind is through a study of one of its most luminous product—metaphor. The goal of this chapter is to look more closely at this remarkable insight, with reference to the fascinating research in CMT.

Concepts

Realizing that they could not gain access to human thinking directly, the ancient Greek philosophers formulated the notion of *concept* to make the study a more tractable and realizable one. But defining what a concept is proved to be (and continues to be) problematic. To see why this is so, take, for example, the concept encoded by the word *cat*. How do we come to know what a cat is? When we look up the definition of *cat* in a dictionary we will find something such as "a carnivorous mammal (*Felis catus*) domesticated since early times as a catcher of rats and mice and as a pet and existing in several distinctive breeds and varieties." The problem with this definition is that it uses *mammal* to define *cat*. What is a *mammal*? The dictionary defines *mammal* as "any of various warm-blooded vertebrate *animals* of the class Mammalia." What is an *animal*? The dictionary goes on to define an *animal* as "a living *organism* other than a plant or a bacterium." What is an *organism*? An *organism*, the dictionary stipulates, is "an individual animal or plant having diverse organs and parts that function together as a whole to maintain *life* and its activities." But, then, what is *life*? *Life*, it specifies, is "the property that distinguishes living *organisms*." At that point the dictionary has gone into a loop—it has employed an already-used concept, *organism*, to define *life*.

Such looping is caused by the fact that dictionaries employ words, which encode concepts, to define an entry. But, here's the paradox—as it turns out, the dictionary approach to definition is the only possible one. Human knowledge has a *de facto* looping associative structure. This suggests that the meaning of something can only be inferred by relating it to the meaning of something else to which it is, or can be, associated. There simply is no such thing as an "absolute concept." So, the meaning of *cat* is something that can only be extrapolated from the associated concepts that it evokes. In addition to the concepts of *mammal, animal, organism,* and *life,* used by the dictionary, one can add others such as *whiskers, retractile claws,* and *tail* to the looping structure of the *cat* concept.

Conceptual knowledge is not an innate feature of the mind—as Plato and Descartes believed (chapter 1). Like other animals, human infants come to understand things in the world at first with their senses, not through any mental apparatus consisting of innate forms or ideas. When they grasp objects, for instance, they are discovering the tactile properties of things; when they put objects in their mouths, they are probing their gustatory properties; and so on. However, in a remarkably short period of time, they start replacing sensory knowing with conceptual knowing—i.e., with words, pictures, and other forms that stand for things. This event is extraordinary—all children require to set their conceptual mode of knowing in motion is simple exposure to concepts in social context through language, pictures, and other kinds of symbol-based systems of representation and communication. From that point on, they require their sensory apparatus less and less to gain knowledge, becoming more and more dependent on their conceptual mode.

The shift from sensory to conceptual knowing was examined empirically in the twentieth century by two brilliant psychologists—Jean Piaget (1896–1980) and Lev S. Vygotsky (1896–1934). Piaget's work documented the presence of a "timetable" in human development that characterizes the shift (Piaget 1923, 1936, 1945, 1955, 1969; Inhelder and Piaget 1958). During the initial stage infants explore the world around them with their senses, but are capable of distinguishing meaningful (sign-based) stimuli (such as verbal ones) from random noises. In short time, they show the ability to carry out simple problem-solving tasks (such as matching colors). Piaget called this the "pre-operational" stage, since it is during this phase that children start to "operate" such concept-based tasks. By the age of 7, which Piaget called the "concrete operations" stage, children become sophisticated thinkers, possessing full language and other conceptual modes of knowing for carrying out complicated tasks. The mental development of human beings culminates in a "formal operations" stage at puberty, when the ability to reason and actualize complex cognitive tasks emerges.

As insightful as Piaget's work is, it makes no reference to the use of metaphor in childhood as a creative strategy for knowing the world. Vygotsky (1962), on the other hand, saw metaphor as a vital clue to understanding the conceptual mode of knowing. When children do not know how to label something—such as the *moon*—they resort to metaphor, calling it a "ball" or a "circle." Such "metaphorical fables," as Vygotsky called them, allow children to interconnect their observations and reflections in a holistic and meaningful fashion. Gradually, these are replaced by the words they acquire in context, which mediate and regulate their thoughts, actions, and behaviors from then on. By the time of puberty children have, in fact, become creatures of their culture—its habits are their habits, its beliefs their beliefs, its challenges their challenges, its rituals their rituals, and so on and so forth. Vygotsky thus saw culture as an "organizing system" of the concepts that originate and develop with a group of people tied together by force of history. To grasp what Vygotsky probably meant, an analogy can be used. A bibliophile may have, over the years, acquired thousands of books on every subject and by every author imaginable. Stockpiling them in a random fashion, however, would make it a time-consuming and clumsy chore for the bibliophile to locate a particular book. To make retrieval more efficient, the bibliophile will have to *organize* the books in some systematic fashion: e.g., put them in alphabetical order on shelves according to author, arrange them in subject categories and then alphabetize them according to author within each category, and so on. Each arrangement constitutes an "organizing system" that allows the bibliophile to retrieve specific books for utilization. Analogously, culture constitutes an organizing system of concepts that allows a group of people living together to retrieve any concept that they might need for efficient utilization.

The study of concept-formation has been a major area of concern for developmental psychology since Piaget and Vygotsky published their significant findings. Among the many psychological theories that have since come forward, *prototype theory* crystallizes as one of the most interesting ones for the purposes of this book. The theory traces its origin to 1958, when the psychologist Roger Brown (1958a) argued that children use what they know in concrete terms in order to refer to something in general—the same basic process inherent in metaphor. For example, Brown found that the word *dime* was used by most of his child subjects to refer both to the general concept of *money* and to specific types of dimes (e.g., a *2003 dime*). Brown referred to *dime* as a prototypical concept, to *money* as a superordinate concept, and to a *2003 dime* as a subordinate concept:

Superordinate Concept = General Category
money
▼
Prototypical Concept = Most Common Manifestation of the Category
dime
▼
Subordinate Concept = Specific Type within the Category
2003 dime

The follow-up research on prototypicality theory has largely confirmed Brown's claim that children learn abstract concepts at the prototypical level and that, in general, prototypicality guides conceptual development (e.g., Rosch 1973a, 1973b, 1975a, 1975b, 1981; Rosch and Mervis 1975; Smith 1988; Taylor 1995). This finding applies as well to linguistic concepts, as the work in *markedness theory* has also shown (Brakel 1983; Andrews 1990; Battistella 1990; Andrews and Tobin 1996). Certain grammatical and lexical categories are perceived as more typical than others to speakers of a language. For instance, the form *a* in English is perceived to be the one that best represents the entire indefinite article category. It is thus called "unmarked;" whereas *an*, which occurs in front of vowels, is called the "marked" form within the category. A marked form occurs less frequently. As a consequence, when it does occur, it carries specific information along with it. For example, in Italian the masculine gender of nouns is the unmarked form in the plural. Thus, in a phrase such as *i turisti americani* ("American tourists") the tourists referred to can be either male or female. On the other hand, when the feminine form is used—*le turiste americane*—then the tourists referred to are only and specifically female.

The foregoing discussion is not meant to imply that the study of concept-formation is a modern-day enterprise. On the contrary, the ancient Greek philosophers had actually come to a truly insightful understanding of concept-formation over two and a half millennia ago. Basically, they claimed that many concepts are formed in one of two fundamental ways—by *induction* or by *deduction*. The former involves reaching a general conclusion from observing a recurring pattern; the latter involves reasoning about the consistency or concurrence of a recurring pattern. Aware that other types of concepts existed (as those found in poetry, the arts, music, etc.), they argued that induction and deduction were particularly apt in explaining logical and mathematical thinking. Take, for example, the fact that the number of degrees in a triangle is $180°$. One way to arrive at knowledge of this fact is, simply, to measure the angles of hundreds, perhaps thousands, of triangles and then observe if a pattern emerges from the measurements. Assuming that the measuring devices are precise and that errors are not made, we are bound to come to the conclusion that the sum of the three angles adds consistently up to $180°$. This "generalization-by-extrapolation" process is the sum and substance of inductive thinking.

The expert mathematician would, however, claim that such thinking is not 100% reliable, because one can never be sure that some triangle may not crop up whose angles add up to more or less than $180°$. To be sure that $180°$ is the sum for *all* triangles one must use a deductive method of demonstration. This inheres in applying already-proved concepts to the case-at-hand. First, a triangle is constructed with the base extended and a line parallel to the base going through its top vertex (A). Angles that form at the vertex are labeled with letters, as shown below:

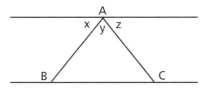

It is an established fact of plane geometry that the angles on opposite sides of a transversal are equal. A transversal is a line that meets two parallel lines. In the diagram above, both **AB** and **AC** are transversals (in addition to being sides of the triangle). We use the known fact to label the equal angles with the same letters:

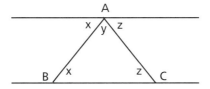

Now, we can use another established fact to show that the angles inside the triangle add up to $180°$—namely, that a straight line is an angle of $180°$. If we look at the parallel line going through **A**, we can see that the sum of the angles at **A** is $x + y + z$. Since these make up a straight line, we now can assert that $x + y + z = 180°$. Next, we look at the angles within the triangle and notice that the sum of these, too, add up to $x + y + z$. Since we know that this sum is equal to $180°$, we have, in effect, proven that the sum of the angles in the triangle is $180°$. Since, the triangle chosen was a general one, because x, y, and z can take on any value we so desire (less than $180°$ of course), we have proven the pattern true for *all* triangles. This "generalization-by-demonstration" process is the sum and substance of deductive thinking.

Induction and deduction do, clearly, play a significant role in the formation of some kinds of concepts. But they hardly explain how the entire range of human concepts comes about. In mathematics itself, moreover, hunches and guesses play a much more central role in the origination of mathematical ideas than is often assumed. It was Charles Peirce (chapter 1), himself a mathematician and logician, who emphasized that many, if not most, of our originating concepts are formed by a type of inferential process that he called *abduction*. He described it as follows (Peirce 1931–1958, V:180):

The abductive suggestion comes to us like a flash. It is an act of *insight*, although of extremely fallible insight. It is true that the different elements of the hypothesis were in our minds before; but it is the idea of putting together what we had never before dreamed of putting together which flashes the new suggestion before our contemplation.

To grasp how insight thinking unfolds, consider the following classic puzzle.

Without letting your pencil leave the paper,
draw four straight lines through the following nine dots:

Many people will approach this puzzle at first by attempting to join up the dots as if they were located on the perimeter (boundary) of a square:

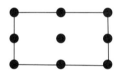

But this reading of the puzzle does not yield a solution, no matter how many times one tries to draw four straight lines without the pencil leaving the paper, as readers can verify for themselves. It is at this point that insight thinking comes into play: "If it is seemingly impossible to join up the dots with four lines, what would happen if one went beyond the imaginary square boundary?" That hunch turns out, in fact, to be the relevant insight leading to a solution.

We start by putting the pencil on, say, the bottom left dot, tracing a straight line upward and stopping when it is in line diagonally with the two dots below it. We could start with any of the four corner dots and produce a solution (as readers can discover for themselves):

Next, we join the two dots (without raising the pencil) by tracing a straight line diagonally downward through them, stopping when our second trace is in horizontal alignment with the three dots along the bottom:

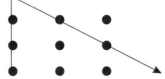

A third line can now be drawn horizontally, from right to left, joining the three dots on the bottom:

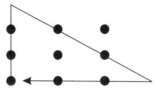

Finally, with a fourth diagonal line, the two remaining dots can be joined:

Clearly, as this puzzle shows, insight thinking involves a guessing process that comes to us as a "flash," as Peirce characterized it. It puts on display the sum and substance of abductive thinking. Most mathematical discoveries come about in this way, not by inductive or deductive reasoning. The latter two are useful as conceptual strategies for consolidating the discoveries made by insight thinking: i.e., they allow for mathematical discoveries to be organized into systems of mathematical knowledge. Once an insight is attained, it becomes useful to "routinize" it, so that a host of related problems can be solved as a matter of course, with little time-consuming mental effort. Such routinization is a memory-preserving and time-saving strategy. It is the rationale behind all organized knowledge systems. Such systems produce *algorithms*—routinized procedures—for solving problems that would otherwise require insight thinking to be used over and over again. Once such thinking has done its job, so to speak, the rational part of the mind steps in to give its products form and stability through other forms of systematic thinking. So, for instance, the above puzzle can now be made to be as complex as we desire (increasing the number of dots to 16, 25, etc.), but the "principle" learned from solving the original puzzle need not be discovered over and over again each time. Rather, we can now use a form of inductive (or perhaps even deductive) thinking to generalize a strategy for solving any puzzle of this type—no matter how many dots are involved.

Sense Implication

A question that also intrigued the ancient Greek philosophers was the following one: How can the difference between a concrete concept such as *stage*, and an abstract one such as *life*, be explained? As we saw in the previous chapter, Aristotle had unwittingly answered this very question by discovering metaphor, but he did not pursue his own discovery —a pretermission that led to the neglect of metaphor for centuries thereafter.

Basically, metaphor is an abduction—the result of associating certain concrete and abstract concepts to each other, not by a pure flight of fancy, but because they entail or implicate each other. Thus, the concept of *life* implicates the concept of a *stage* and, vice versa, *stages* implicate the concept of *life* because of what occurs on them. This type of "bi-directional" entailment can be called the *Sense Implication Hypothesis* (SIH) (Sebeok and Danesi 2000). As an example of how sense implication operates at a practical cognitive level, take the word *blue* in English. As a concrete concept, *blue* was probably extrapolated from observing a pattern of hue found in natural phenomena such as the sky and the sea, and then by noting the occurrence of the same hue in other things. The specific image of *blue* that comes to mind will, of course, be different from individual to individual. But all images will fall within a certain hue range on the light spectrum. In a phrase, the word *blue* allows speakers of English to talk and think about the occurrence of a specific hue in a concrete way. But that is not all it does. Speakers use the very same concept to characterize emotions, morals, and other abstractions. Consider, for instance, the two sentences below:

1. Today I've got the *blues*.
2. That piece of information hit me right out of the *blue*.

The use of *blue* in (1) to mean "sad" or "gloomy" is the result of a culture-specific sense-implication process, coming out of the tradition of "blues" music. The latter is perceived typically to evoke sadness or melancholy through its melodies, harmonies, rhythms, and lyrics. The use of *blue* in (2) to render the concept of "unexpectedness" comes, instead, out of the tradition of ascribing unpredictability to the weather, symbolized by a *blue sky*. Upon closer examination, such uses belong to metaphorical traditions—the former is an instantiation of the conceptual metaphor that connects *mood* with *color* and the latter of the conceptual metaphor that connects *destiny* with *Nature*, which literary critics classify under the rubric of *pathetic fallacy*. These two sense linkages underlie the conceptual structure of the above two sentences and, indeed, of many other common expressions such as the following:

mood is a facial color

3.   She turned *red* with embarrassment.

4.   My cousin is *green* with envy.

Nature is a portent of destiny

5.   I heard it from an *angry wind*.

6.   *Cruel clouds* are gathering over the world.

Examples such as these show that concrete and abstract concepts implicate each other through an entailment based on sense. As anthropologist Roger Wescott (1980) has amply documented, color vocabularies seem in fact to have originated through such entailment, i.e., through an association of hues with natural and human events. In the ancient Hittite language, for instance, words for colors initially designated plants and trees such as *poplar*, *elm*, *cherry*, *oak*, etc.; in Hebrew, the name of the first man, *Adam*, meant *red* and *alive*, and still today, in languages of the Slavic family, *red* signifies *living* and *beautiful*. In effect, Wescott has shown that in many languages (perhaps in most) the names for colors were forged as metaphors—a tendency that is still manifest in how we label certain emotions to this day: e.g., *browned off* ("annoyed"), which may have a fecal source; *tickled pink* ("pleased"), which may have been motivated by the perception that stimulated pale skin produces a pleasant effect; and so on and so forth.

Consider, more specifically, the color *red*, which is associated with "blood" and thus "vitality." In many languages, the naming of "red" co-occurred with the naming of "blood," leaving a residue in many symbolic practices. In tribal and cult-based rituals, for instance, it is common to slit the wrists of fellow members and rub them together so that they may become *blood brothers*. In the medieval ages, it was commonly believed that love was a sickness that could be cured by bleeding people. Such examples provide evidence that we grasp abstract concepts by associating them to concrete qualities and, vice versa, that we grasp concrete concepts by extrapolating them from abstract notions.

Consider, as another example, the word *tail*, which the dictionary defines as "the flexible appendage found at the rear end of an animal's body." This is the concrete meaning of *tail* in utterances such as the following:

7.   My cat's *tail* is nearly one foot long.

8.   Are there any species of dogs without *tails*?

9.   That horse's *tail* is rather short, isn't it?

The association of *tail* with *appendages* and *rear-ends* provides basic information about what a *tail* is—an extremity—and where it is found —on a rear-end. Now, it is these physical properties that guide the use of the word *tail* as a means for understanding a host of other concepts:

10. The *tail* of that shirt is rather crumpled.
11. Do you want heads or *tails* for this coin toss?
12. The *tail* section of that airplane is making a funny noise.

Shirts, coins, and *airplanes* are said to have *tails* because they are perceived to have appendages and rear-ends. It is irrelevant if the appendage is on an animal or an object—it is still a *tail* conceptually. Although it is not the actual physical qualities of animal tails that are envisioned in *shirts, coins,* and the like, these qualities are nonetheless implicated by suggestion.

The SIH provides a tentative framework for understanding a host of conceptual subtleties that would otherwise go unexplained. Take, for example the *people are animals* conceptual metaphor (chapter 1). Using prototype theory (above), this can now be defined as a superordinate (i.e,. general) metaphorical idea. The choice of *snake* from the *animal* source domain, produces a basic personality concept: e.g., *John is a snake.* However, if we want to refine our metaphorical portrait, then we can construct subordinate metaphorical concepts that allow us to zero in on specific details of personality:

13. He's a *cobra.*
14. She's a *viper.*
15. Your friend is a *boa constrictor.*

In so doing, we are thus able to modulate our descriptions of personality in ways that parallel our sensory reactions to each type of snake. This suggests that what are called *domains* in CMT are themselves products of the process of sense implication—the target domain *(personality)* implicates a specific kind of source domain *(animals),* which, in turn, implicates certain subdomains *(types of animals)* which, in their turn, suggest other subdomains *(types of snake),* and so on. The domains are not autonomous regions of human mentation. They are linked through sense implication. Vico was probably the first to understand this very fact of concept-formation:

> It is noteworthy that in all languages the greater part of the expressions relating to inanimate things are formed by metaphor from the human body and its parts and from the human senses and passions...All of which is a consequence of our axiom ...that man in his ignorance makes himself the rule of the universe, for in the examples cited he has made of himself an en-

41

tire world. So that, as rational metaphysics teaches that man becomes all things by understanding them…this imaginative metaphysics shows that man becomes all things by not understanding them…and perhaps the latter proposition is truer than the former, for when man understands he extends his mind and takes in the things, but when he does not understand he makes the things out of himself and becomes them by transforming himself into them (Bergin and Fisch 1984, 129–130).

Given the controversy surrounding the term *association* in psychology and linguistics, it is necessary at this point to clarify, albeit schematically, what I mean by it as used in this book. In psychology, *associationism* is the theory that the mind comes to form concepts by combining simple, irreducible elements through mental connection. One of the first to utilize the notion of association was Aristotle, who identified four strategies by which associations are forged: by similarity (e.g., an orange and a lemon), difference (e.g., hot and cold), contiguity in time (e.g., sunrise and a rooster's crow), and contiguity in space (e.g., a cup and saucer). British empiricist philosophers John Locke (1690) and David Hume (1749) saw sensory perception as the underlying factor in guiding the associative process; i.e., things that are perceived to be similar or contiguous in time or space are associated to each other; those that are not are kept distinct. In the nineteenth century, the early psychologists, guided by the principles enunciated by James Mill (1773–1836) in his *Analysis of the Phenomena of the Human Mind* (1829), studied experimentally how subjects made associations. In addition to Aristotle's original four strategies, they found that factors such as intensity, inseparability, and repetition played a role in associative processes: e.g., arms are associated with bodies because they are inseparable from them; rainbows are associated with rain because of repeated observations of the two as co-occurring phenomena; etc.

The early psychologists had, in effect, unwittingly established the validity of the SIH as the basis for making associations. However, associationism took a different route when Ivan Pavlov (1849–1936) published his famous experiments with dogs (Pavlov 1902). When Pavlov presented a meat stimulus to a hungry dog, the animal would salivate spontaneously, as expected. He termed this the dog's "unconditioned response"—an instinctual response programmed into each species by Nature. After Pavlov rang a bell while presenting the meat stimulus a number of times, he found that the dog would eventually salivate only to the ringing bell, without the meat stimulus. Clearly, Pavlov suggested, the ringing by itself, which would not have triggered the salivation initially, had brought about a "conditioned response" in the dog. It was thus by repeated association of the bell with the meat stimulus that the dog had learned something new—something not based on instinctual understanding. Every major behavioral school of psychology has utilized the Pavlovian notion of conditioning in one way or other. To this day, behaviorists believe that the learning of new material can, by and large, be accounted for as the result of conditioned associations between stimuli and responses. Psychologists of other schools, however, reject this type of associationism as useless when it comes to explaining different kinds of learning, such as problem-solving.

In my view, the Pavlovian notion of conditioning is still a useful one on many counts, despite the many questions it raises. However, it does not in any way explain how concepts beget their meanings in relation to other concepts. The evidence coming out of the CMT research field suggests that such meanings crystallize through sense implication, thus corroborating the early work on associationism. The pervasiveness of metaphor in concept-formation suggests that our brain is a *de facto* association-making organ. The very fact that even models of metaphor are, *necessarily*, metaphors themselves bears this out. It is hopeless to talk about anything theoretically without recourse to metaphor, as may have become obvious to the reader of this book by now. As Edie (1976, 193) has appropriately remarked, it is "impossible to understand the human mind or human behavior except by making a metaphorical detour."

Sense implication is not a monolithic process. It varies in the type and degree of the implication. Consider the concept of *anger*. Because anger entails certain specific kinds of bodily reactions, such as an increase in muscle tension, our conceptualization of *anger* will betray these very reactions—*bodily temperature, redness,* etc.—in some physical way and to some degree. This is why concepts such as *boiling, redness,* etc. are used in metaphorical expressions used to deliver the concept of *anger* in common discourse:

16. I'm *boiling* with anger.
17. Don't be so angry; you're face is *red*.

In such cases the implication is, obviously, of a sensory nature. However, in many others it is more intellectual than it is sensory. Consider, as an example, the metaphorical uses of the word *house*. As a concrete concept, the word denotes "any (free-standing) structure intended for human habitation." This meaning can be seen in utterances such as *I bought a new house yesterday, House prices are continually going up in this city, We repainted our house the other day,* and so on. The basic image schema implicated is that of a "container of human beings." Now, it is this image that is implicated in the use of *house* in the following expressions:

18. The *house* is in session.
19. The *house* roared with laughter.

20. They sleep at one of the *houses* at Harvard.

The *house* concept can, in effect, be used to refer to anything that implicates humans coming together in some "container" for some specific reason; i.e., by implication audiences, legislative assemblies, and dormitories imply "container structures" of special kinds that humans can be said to occupy in some specific way. So, when we say that *This university houses some great thinkers* the image of a house as a "human container" is implicated by intellectual sense.

Sense-implication can also be guided or constrained by cultural practices and traditions. Consider, as a case-in-point, how the naming of the third game in a three-game series in baseball came into existence. If one team wins the first game and the other the second game, then the third game is called the *rubber match* of the series. On the other hand, if one team wins the first two games, then the third game is designated differently—the winning team is said to *go for the sweep* in that game and the losing team is said to attempt to *avoid the sweep*. The sense implication in this case is one dictated by historical practices rather than strict sensory entailment.

The foregoing discussion makes it obvious that concept-formation is, essentially, an imaginative process based on sense-making. The great American philosopher Susanne Langer (1948, 129) compared it, appropriately, to a "fantasy:"

> Suppose a person sees, for the first time in his life, a train arriving at a station. He probably carries away what we should call a "general impression" of noise and mass. Very possibly he has not noticed the wheels going round, but only the rods moving like a runner's knees. He does not instantly distinguish smoke from steam, nor the hissing from the squeaking. Yet the next time he watches a train pull in the process is familiar. His mind retains a fantasy which "means" the general concept, "a train arriving at a station." Everything that happens the second time is, to him like or unlike the first time. The fantasy…was abstracted from the very first instance, and made the later ones "familiar."

Needless to say, what has been called the SIH here is not a universally accepted theory of concept-formation. One diametrically opposite view is that concept-based processes are determined by innate structures. Linguistic concepts, for instance, are said to emerge as the result of innate principles of grammar built into the brain. To account for differences in languages, the congener of this view, Chomsky (chapter 1), has proposed the notion of "parameters," which he defines as organizational subprinciples within the brain's Universal Grammar (UG) that allow a specific language to take shape from simple exposure to it (Chomsky

1986, 2000, 2002). But what is a parameter? To equate the actual grammatical rules of a language with parameters is the equivalent of equating a melody with the notes written on a page to represent it. The question of what is a melody psychologically would still remain unanswered. Similarly, the question of what is a parameter cannot be circumvented by simply writing a rule and then claiming that it is an instantiation of a parameter. Such a claim would be no more than a case of *post hoc ergo propter hoc* reasoning ("after this, therefore because of this"). More will be said about UG theory in subsequent chapters. Suffice it to say here that it comes as no surprise to find that it excludes metaphor from its purview for a simple reason—metaphor is the proverbial "fly in the theoretical ointment" of UG theory. No wonder, then, that Chomsky has characterized metaphor, like Hobbes and Locke before him, as a "fault" of linguistic behavior—a characterization that smacks more of defensiveness and territoriality than it does of anything else.

Brain Research

The SIH is really no more than a "psychological term" that attempts to encapsulate how poetic logic operates psychologically and neurologically. As such, it is intended to suggest that the brain itself is a "poetic" organ in the Vichian sense. Now, the question becomes: Is there any empirical evidence to support the SIH? As it turns out, there is plenty of it, although it is scattered in various subfields of investigation.

Neuroscience has established that the left hemisphere (LH) of the brain is the primary locus for language, distributed mainly in three subregions: (1) *Broca's area* lying just beneath the motor cortex, which is responsible for the muscle movements of the throat and mouth while speaking; (2) *Wernicke's area*, between the auditory and visual areas, which controls linguistic comprehension; and (3) a *supplementary area* discovered by the Canadian neurologist Wilder Penfield and his associates in the 1950s (Penfield and Rasmussen 1950; Penfield and Roberts 1959), which is involved in several functions previously thought to be located in Broca's and Wernicke's areas. However, this neurological classification of the language functions hardly tells the whole story. Already in the 1930s, the Russian psychologist Vygotsky (above) argued that the view of language as a strictly left-hemispheric function was a highly restrictive one. While it is true that phonetic and grammatical functions may have a primary locus in the LH, as a communicative-expressive tool language is more likely to arise from the interaction of neural structures that are distributed throughout the brain. Vygotsky suggested, moreover, that the whole brain, not just one hemisphere, was endowed at birth with a unique kind of "plasticity" that rendered it highly sensitive and adaptive to changes and influences during childhood. In the formation of color concepts, for instance, Vygotsky showed experimentally that the neuronal structures in the RH, which are involved in the perception of hue, interact with those in the LH when color terms are learned by children. This suggests a "right-to-left" shift in concept-formation. The main reason for this shift seems to be the anatomical structure of the two hemispheres. The greater connectivity it has with other centers in the complex neuronal pathways of the brain makes the RH a better distributor of new information. The LH, on the other hand, has a more sequentially-organized neuronal structure and, thus, finds it more difficult to assimilate information for which no previous categories exist.

New technologies such as *Positron Emission Tomography* (PET) scanning and *Functional Magnetic Resonance Imaging* (fMRI) now make it possible for neuroscientists to observe the brain directly while people speak, listen, read, and think, because they produce images similar to X-rays that show which parts of the brain are active while a person carries out a particular mental or physical task. The PET and fMRI studies have largely confirmed Vygotsky's hypothesis that concept-formation is "interhemispheric." Moreover, it now appears certain that different types of language tasks activate different areas of the brain in diverse sequences and patterns. The fMRI research has also detected the activation of the emotional areas of the brain during language use. The limbic system, which includes portions of the temporal lobes, parts of the hypothalamus and thalamus, and other structures, may thus have a larger role than previously thought in the processing of speech and in the formation of concepts (Damasio 1994). Research of this kind clearly supports the SIH, since it claims, essentially, that sensory and emotional processes are implicated in the formation of concepts of all kinds, especially metaphorical ones.

The sense-implicative connectivity that characterizes human thinking has been examined not only experimentally with human subjects, but also theoretically with computer software. Computer models of brain functioning are called *Parallel Distributed Processing* (PDP) models (Rumelhart and McClelland 1986). These are designed to show how, potentially, neural networks form linkages with each other in the processing of information. The PDP models are believed to perform the same kinds of tasks and operations that complex functions such as language does (MacWhinney 2000). As Obler and Gjerlow (1999, 11) put it, the research on PDP models has shown that in all probability "there are no language centers per se but rather 'network nodes' that are stimulated; eventually one of these is stimulated enough that it passes a certain threshold and that node is 'realized,' perhaps as a spoken word."

One finding that stands out and is particularly relevant to the present discussion is that metaphor originates in the RH—a finding that predates the PET and fMRI research, coming out of the study of brain-damaged patients. In 1964, for instance, Weinstein demonstrated that patients with RH damage had lost the ability to comprehend and produce metaphors. Following that study, in 1977 Ellen Winner and Howard Gardner presented a series of pictures to brain-damaged subjects who were asked to select one of four captions that best portrayed the meaning of each picture. For the caption *A heavy heart can really make a difference* the subjects were shown four pictures from which to choose: (1) a person crying (= metaphorical meaning); (2) a person staggering under the weight of a huge red heart (= literal meaning); (3) a 500-pound weight (= a representation emphasizing the adjective *heavy*); (4) a red heart (= a representation emphasizing the noun phrase *red heart*). The subjects were divided into those with LH damage, those with RH damage, and a normal control group. Normals and LH subjects gave up to five times as many metaphorical responses; but the RH group showed great difficulty in coming up with the appropriate metaphorical answers. Winner and Gardner thus established a link between the meaning of a metaphor and the RH of the brain, suggesting that metaphor and mental imagery are intertwined.

In the same year, Stachowiak, Huber, Poeck, and Kerschensteiner (1977) read subjects brief stories and then asked them to pick from a set of five drawings the one which best described what happened to the main character of a story. The groups tested were LH patients, RH patients, and normals. The researchers found that, of the three groups, the RH patients were the ones who showed the most difficulty in processing metaphorical drawings, thus complementing Winner and Gardner's findings. In the 1980s the evidence in favor of a RH involvement in metaphor had become extensive. Hier and Kaplan (1980), for instance, found that RH patients exhibited deficits in explaining the meaning of proverbs. Wapner, Hamby, and Gardner (1981) discovered that RH patients tended to exhibit significant difficulty in deriving the moral of a story, offering, in general, a nonsensical literal interpretation—a finding confirmed by Brownell, Potter, and Michelow (1984); Brownell (1988); and Bottini et al. (1994).

The work in neuroscience has thus largely confirmed that the brain produces metaphor by synthesizing the sense-implicative properties of the RH with the more verbal and analytical ones of the LH. Conceptualization, it would seem, is a product of the "body in the mind" as Johnson (1987) has aptly phrased it, and as Vico certainly knew over two and a half decades ago. Foreshadowing modern day research, Vico claimed that we think in sensory images before giving verbal substance to our thoughts. He called these "imaginative universals" (Bergin and Fisch 1984, 204–210, 403, 809, 933–934). In early humanity, these images constituted the basis of the first concepts, which were formed typically as gods or heroes. The ancient Egyptians, for instance, formed the concept of "civil wisdom" through the figure of Thrice-Great Hermes (Bergin and Fisch 1984, 209); the Greeks formed the concept of "valor" through the character of Achilles (Bergin and Fisch 1984, 403), and so on. Children, Vico went on to suggest, acquire concepts in exactly the same way, through god-like and heroic story characters who embody them—an observation to which we can still relate to this day.

Layering

The activation of the two hemispheres in the production of metaphor implies, in strict psychological terms, that concept-formation is intertwined with perception and imagery. According to some linguists, this "imagery-to-concept" flow in conceptualization characterizes all of language. Langacker (1987, 7) summarizes this perspective as follows:

> Linguistic expressions and grammatical constructions embody conventional imagery, which constitutes an essential aspect of their semantic value. In choosing a particular expression or construction, a speaker construes the conceived situation in a certain way, i.e. he selects one particular image (from a range of alternatives) to structure its conceptual content for expressive purposes.

The central notion in CMT is, in fact, that "conventional imagery" guides the construction of metaphorical models. When we hear people talking, for instance, of *ideas* in terms of *circles, points,* etc., we can easily identify the type of imagery they are deploying as *geometrical figures/ relations:*

21. Don't you think those ideas are *circular?*
22. I don't see the *point* you are making.
23. Her ideas are *central* to the discussion.
24. Their ideas are *diametrically* opposite.
25. Those ideas are *parallel.*
26. My idea is in *line* with yours.

As mentioned in the previous chapter, Lakoff and Johnson (1980) were probably the first language scientists to characterize such expressions as instantiations of a more general thought formula **A is B**, where **A** is called the target domain and **B** the source domain—*ideas* (**A**) *are geometrical figures/relations* (**B**). Lakoff and Johnson explained the formation of such formulas (called conceptual metaphors) as a process dependent upon image schemata that have become largely unconscious in speakers of a language for the simple reason that they have become habits of thought. However, the specific type of schema implicated in the above conceptual metaphor (a line, a circle, etc.) will manifest itself explicitly when someone is asked, for example, to draw a "visual model" of an idea or a theory. In such a case, the person will tend to draw the model as if it consisted of lines, circles, etc. Flow charts in computer programming are cases-in-point of the use of geometrical image schemata to model something abstract. The image schemata also come out in the gesture forms that speakers make when they deliver the above expressions orally: e.g.; when people speak of *ideas* as being *circular*, they tend to make a circular gesture as they speak; similarly, when they speak of *ideas* as being *parallel* they tend to put one hand over the other in a parallel way. More will be said about the relation between such representations and metaphor in subsequent chapters. Suffice it to say here that they are "reifications" of the imagery content built into metaphorical expressions.

To get a firmer sense of the notion of conceptual metaphor as a thought formula based on image schemata, consider the abstract topic of *argument*. What is an argument? At an experiential level it is something that involves disagreement, dispute, or debate. Every person knows, or more precisely "feels," when he or she is involved in an argument. In attempting to grasp what kinds of feeling structures an argument implicates, speakers of English typically use images based on bellicose or warlike activities. The result is the conceptual metaphor *argument is war*:

27. Your claims are *indefensible*.
28. You *attacked* all my *weak points*.
29. Your criticisms were right *on target*.
30. I *demolished* his argument.
31. I've never *won* an argument.
32. She *shot down* all my points.
33. If you use that *strategy*, I'll *wipe you out*.

What does speaking about arguments in this way imply? It means, as Lakoff and Johnson (1980, 12) suggest, that we actually envision being involved in a "war" when we argue and that we thus feel that we can "win" or "lose" arguments. That is why we say that we can *attack* a position, *lose ground*, *plan* strategy, *defend* or *abandon* a *line of attack*, etc.

Take, as another example, the use of *vision* to conceptualize *ideas* and *understanding* (Wierzbicka 1996, 301):

34. There is more to this than *meets the eye*.
35. I have a different *point of view*.
36. It all depends on how you *look* at it.

37. I take a *dim view* of the whole matter.
38. I never *see eye to eye* on things with you.
39. You have a different *worldview* than I do.
40. Your ideas have given me great *insight* into life.

Now, the remarkable thing is that this very conceptual metaphor suggests by itself a series of related source domains, such as the *light* source domain to deliver the concept of *knowing*. In this case, the physical properties of *light* (visibility, brightness, etc.) implicate *knowing* (in all its variations) as "internal vision." It is a common concept that is used to discuss many types of knowledge in English, such as *awareness, discernment, clarification, purpose, perspective*, etc. (Viberg 1983; Danesi 1990, 2001).

41. I have acted in the *light* of experience.
42. His words shed some *light* on the issue.
43. That newspaper brought the scandal to *light*.
44. He saw the situation in a different *light*.
45. They were guided by the *light* of reason.
46. My grandchildren are the *lights* of my life.
47. She is one of the leading *lights* of the theater.
48. There was a strange *light* in her eyes.

The counterpart to this concept is, of course, *darkness inhibits knowing*. The two complementary concepts manifest themselves in antonymous ways in discourse typically as follows:

49. We have all been *enlightened* by his words.
    vs.
50. His presentation *obscured* the whole issue.

51. That was an age of *enlightenment* in the history of education.
    vs.
52. That was a *dark* age in the history of education.

53. Her explanation *threw light* on the whole matter.
    vs.
54. Her explanation kept us in the *dark*.

55. I see that issue in a different *light* than you do.
    vs.
56. He took a *dark view* of that matter.

57. He brought that issue to *light*.
    vs.
58. He kept that issue hidden in the *dark*.

59. She is a *luminary* in her profession.
    vs.
60. Her work is *obscure*.

61. His intentions are *glowing* ones.
    vs.
62. His intentions appear to be *shadowy*.

There are, actually, numerous concepts that can be derived from the *vision* source domain. One of these, *ideas are viewable objects*, is commonly linked to other source domains to produce increasingly complex metaphorical models of *intellection* and *knowledge*. The following expressions are cases-in-point (Danesi and Santeramo 1995; Fillmore 1997):

63. When did you *think up* that preposterous idea?
64. You should *think over* carefully what you have just said.
65. *Think out* the entire strategy, before deciding what to do.
66. I cannot *think straight* today.
67. Go ahead and *think* that problem *through*.

These expressions are, clearly, instantiations of several vision concepts that have "blended together," to use a term introduced by Fauconnier and Turner (2002). The verb form *think up* (63) elicits a mental image of *ideas* as objects that can be extracted physically upwards from a terrain; *think over* (64) evokes the image of *ideas* as objects that can be scanned with the mind's eye; *think out* (65) elicits the image of *ideas* as objects being taken from a container so that that they can be seen; *think straight* (66) elicits the image of ideas as objects (points) on a linear path; and *think through* (67) evokes the image of *ideas* as objects moving in continuously through space:

- think up =
    ideas are viewable objects + ideas are objects that can be extracted
- think over =
    ideas are viewable objects + ideas are objects that can be scanned
- think out =
    ideas are viewable objects + ideas are objects in a container
- think straight =
    ideas are viewable objects + ideas are points on a line
- think through =
    ideas are viewable objects + ideas are objects in space

These conceptual blends allow speakers to locate and identify abstract ideas in relation to spatiotemporal phenomena, although such phenomena are purely imaginary. They transform the physiology of vision into a "physiology of thought."

The blending of concepts to produce more complex concepts can be called *layering* (Danesi 2001). More will be said about this notion in the fourth chapter. Suffice it to say here that it allows us to analyze concepts as belonging to different levels or layers of metaphorical activity. A first-order layer is one that is constructed with concrete source domains (i.e., with vehicles referring to concrete referents)—a construction that produces the most basic kind of conceptual metaphor (e.g., *thinking is seeing*). A second-order layer is one that is derived from first-order concepts. The expressions above—*think up, think through,* etc.—are second-order concepts since they result from the linkage of two concepts—*ideas are viewable objects + ideas are objects that can be extracted, ideas are viewable objects + ideas are objects that can be scanned*, etc. The third-order metaphorical layer crystallizes from constant amalgams of previously-formed layers. It is a productive source of cultural symbolism, as will be discussed in due course. For example, in order to understand the meaning of *love is a rose* we must first know that *love is a plant* (as in *Love grows* and *My love has deep roots*) and that *love is a sweetness* (as in *She's my sweetheart* and *They're on a honeymoon*). The association of these two conceptual metaphors to each other produces *love is a rose,* since a *rose* is both a *plant* and gives off a *sweet* odor.

Image Schemata

As the foregoing discussion makes obvious, imagery is central to the production and comprehension of metaphor. Aware of this very fact, Lakoff and Johnson put the notion of *image schema* at the center of CMT (Lakoff 1987; Johnson 1987; Lakoff and Johnson 1999), defining it as the mental outline of some recurring figure, event, action, etc. (see also Alverson 1991). Although we do not normally attend to the details of its composition, these can easily be brought to conscious awareness. For example, people would not normally have a conscious image of a [container][1] when they use an expression such as *spill the beans*. However, if they were asked to explain it by answering a question such as *Where are the beans before they are spilled?* then they would tend to answer it in a remarkably uniform way: i.e., they would say that the beans are kept in a

---

1 Note that square brackets, [ ], are used throughout the text to enclose schemas.

container that is about the size of the human head (Lakoff 1987, 444–446).

An image schema can implicate any one of our sensory or emotional modalities. Consider the following expressions:

68. the sound of thunder
69. the feel of wet grass
70. the smell of fish
71. the taste of toothpaste
72. the sensation of being uncomfortably cold
73. the sensation of extreme happiness
74. the glow of the setting sun

The image schema evoked by (68) has an auditory modality, rather than a visual one like the [container] schema. The one elicited by (69) has a tactile modality, by (70) an olfactory one, by (71) a gustatory quality, by (72) a kinetic one, by (73) an emotional one, and by (74) a visual one. Sometimes, several modalities are implicated. As a concrete example, consider the image schema of an [impediment], which has both visual and tactile properties, since impediments or obstacles can be both seen and touched:

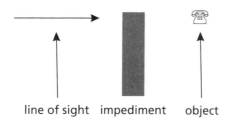

line of sight   impediment   object

Impediment Image Schema

Visually, the schema suggests that we will have to undertake several potential actions in order to get to the object. For example, it suggests that we could go *around* the [impediment], *over* it, *under* it, or *through* it. From a tactile perspective, the schema suggests other kinds of actions should be taken in order to get to the object. For instance, it suggests that we could *remove* the [impediment] and *continue on* towards the object; on the other hand, the [impediment] could successfully *impede* or *block* us, so that we would have to *stop* at it and *turn back*. Now, these are the imaginary actions that guide the formation of various conceptual metaphors, which show that we perceive problems, setbacks, delays, and difficulties of various kinds as "impediments" blocking the attainment of some "object:"

75. Somehow, we *got through* that difficult time.
76. Jim felt better after he *got over* his cold.
77. You need to *steer clear of* financial debt.
78. With the bulk of the work *out of the way*, he was able to call it a day.
79. The rain *stopped* us from enjoying our picnic.
80. You cannot *go any further* with that idea; you'll just have to *turn back*.

Lakoff and Johnson identify several basic types of image schemata. One of these implicates the experience of physical space. This guides the formation of conceptual metaphors such as *happiness is up* (e.g., *I'm feeling up today*) and *sadness is down* (e.g., *They're feeling down today*). A second type implicates the physical qualities of objects, impediments, containers, entities, and substances, which in turn guide the formation of conceptual metaphors such as *the mind is a container* (e.g., *I'm full of memories, I can't keep anything in my mind*, etc.) and *ideas are buildings* (e.g., *That theory is built on a solid foundation*) (Klein 1994). Other types of schemata implicate the same kinds of sensory or perceptual processes as those involved in seeing, breathing, etc. (e.g., *I can't see what you are saying, She's a breath of fresh air*, etc.). Here is a sampling of how such image schemata underlie various concepts:

happiness is up—sadness is down
81. I'm feeling *up* today.
82. She's feeling *down*.
83. His phone call *boosted* my spirits.
84. My mood *sank* after he spoke.
85. That lecture gave me a *lift*.

health and life are up—sickness and death are down
86. I'm at the *peak* of my health.
87. She *fell* ill suddenly, but then got quickly better.
88. Life is an *uphill* struggle.
89. Lazarus *rose* from the dead.
90. Her health is *sinking* fast.

knowledge is light—ignorance is darkness
91. I was *illuminated* by that professor.
92. I was left in the *dark* about what happened.
93. She communicates her ideas very *clearly*.
94. That theory is *obscure*.
95. His example *shed light* on several matters.

ideas are buildings
96. That is a *well-constructed* theory.

97. His ideas are on *solid ground.*
98. That theory needs *support.*
99. Their argument *collapsed* under criticism.
100. She put together the *framework* of a new theory.

ideas are plants

101. Her ideas have finally come to *fruition.*
102. That's a *budding* new theory.
103. Plato's ideas have many contemporary *offshoots.*
104. Trigonometry is a *branch* of mathematics.

ideas are commodities—money

105. He certainly knows how to *package* his ideas.
106. That idea just won't *sell.*
107. There's no *market* for that idea.
108. That's a *worthless* idea.

The reason why we do not consciously detect the presence of image schemata in such common expressions is because of their repeated usage in everyday discourse. For example, we no longer interpret the word *see* in sentences such as *I don't see what you mean, Do you see what I'm saying?* in sense implicative terms, because its metaphorical utilization has become so familiar to us. But the association between the biological act of seeing outside the body and the imaginary act of seeing within mind-space was the original source of such expressions.

What Is the Mind?

An implicit theme that I have attempted to interlace throughout this chapter is that it is impossible to study the mind without recourse to metaphor. As Vico put it, the only way we have of understanding the mind is through sense implication: "The human mind is naturally inclined by the senses to see itself externally in the body" (in Bergin and Fisch 1984, 236).

Sense-implication, as mentioned, is a psychological term for poetic logic. Vico sought access to the workings of poetic logic, not by means of a method of observation and analysis, but through a study of metaphor and myth. For Vico, Descartes's "spectator theory" of knowledge was of little value, for he did not believe reality could be studied independently of the individual's involvement in it. As an alternative to Descartes's *cogito ergo sum* ("I think therefore I am") perspective, Vico proposed one by which humans first feel, then vaguely perceive what they have felt, and, finally, attempt to develop distinct ideas from their perceptions. So, in counterposition to Descartes's maxim, Vico's perspective can be phrased as *sentio ergo sum* ("I feel therefore I am").

In *Book Two* of the *New Science*, Vico suggested that the mind is indistinguishable from metaphor, which he characterized as a "fable in brief:"

> All the first tropes are corollaries of this poetic logic. The most luminous and therefore the most necessary and frequent is metaphor. It is most praised when it gives sense and passion to insensate things, in accordance with the metaphysics above discussed, by which the first poets attributed to bodies the being of animate substances, with capacities measured by their own, namely sense and passion, and in this way made fables of them. Thus every metaphor so formed is a fable in brief (in Bergin and Fisch 1984, 404).

Metaphorical thinking is thus the "default" form of thinking. Rationality, Vico conceded, is humanity's greatest achievement. But, unlike rationalist philosophers, he did not see it as an innate faculty of mind. Rather, he saw it as a *forma mentis* that was achievable only in a social ambiance. Human beings do not inherit rationality from their biological legacy. Stripped of culture, they would be forced to resort to their poetic, or corporeal, imaginations to make sense of the world all over again. The progression from poetic to rational forms of cognition seems to be built into the structure of the brain. This progression, Vico argued, is mirrored in the etymology of our words, symbols, and artifacts. These are mementos of the ideas and theories of the world that we have come up with, shaping what Bonner (1980, 186) calls "true culture" as the "system of representing all the subtleties of language."

Chapter 3

LANGUAGE

Without words to objectify and
categorize our sensations and
place them in relation to one
another, we cannot evolve a
tradition of what is real in the world.
— Ruth Hubbard (1924–)

As the basis for constructing and encoding knowledge, language is truly a wondrous achievement. Without it, human civilization, as we know it, would disappear. The knowledge preserved in books (in paper or electronic form), and to which anyone can have access if one knows the appropriate languages in which the books were written, constitutes the intellectual scaffold of human history, sustaining social and technological growth. It is no exaggeration to say that if all the books in the world, in whatever medium they are constructed, were to be destroyed overnight, human beings would have to start all over reinventing civilization. Writers, scientists, educators, lawmakers, etc. would have to come together to literally "rewrite" knowledge.

There is no more effective way for classifying the world than through words. These allow a group of speakers to label and, thus, organize those aspects of reality that are felt to be meaningful to them. As a consequence, words also make it possible for people to summon up past events, to refer to incidents that have not as yet occurred, to formulate questions about existence, to answer them, to conjure up fictional worlds, and to give thoughts and actions a preservable form. No wonder, then, that questions of what language is, how it originated, and what role it plays in human life are ancient. But such questions are unresolved and may, in fact, never be answered. However, as I will argue in this chapter, investigating the role metaphor plays in the production of linguistic meaning and in shaping grammatical structure will provide some tantalizing clues about how such questions can, at the very least, be approached.

What Is Language?

Above all else, the language spoken by a group of people reveals what kinds of meanings are critical to them, and, as some linguists claim, may even reveal how they view reality. As the American anthropologist Edward Sapir (1884–1939) emphasized throughout his career, we are, essentially, what we speak (Sapir 1921). Sapir's pupil, Benjamin Lee Whorf (1897–1941), went so far as to claim that the thoughts people have are shaped, essentially, by the vocabulary and grammar of the language they speak (Whorf 1956). In effect, if such scholars are right, language is much more than a vehicle for communicating our thoughts, as is commonly thought. It constitutes, rather, a powerful cognitive filter through which we come to view and understand the world.

The Sapir-Whorf hypothesis, as it has come to be called, raises some rather fundamental questions about the relation between language and reality. Do terms such as *chairman* or *spokesman* predispose speakers of English to view some social roles as gender-specific? Feminist social critics seem to think so. They maintain that English grammar is organized from the perspective of those at the power center of the society—the men. That is why, not long ago, speakers of English tended to say that a woman *married into* a man's family; and why, at traditional wedding ceremonies, the marrying cleric would say *I pronounce you man and wife*. Such linguistic habits define women in relation to men. Others, such as *lady atheist* or *lesbian doctor*, are exclusionary of women, since they imply that atheists and doctors are not typically female or lesbian. Needless to say, not all languages are biased towards the male gender. In the Iroquois language, for instance, the reverse is true. The vocabulary, grammar, and discourse protocols of Iroquois reflect a different perspective of things —the female one. The equivalent of *I pronounce you man and wife* in that language would be something like *I pronounce you woman and husband*. This female bias in the language is a result of the fact that in Iroquois society the women are in charge—they hold the land, they pass it on to their heirs in the female line, they are responsible for agricultural production, they control the wealth, they arrange marriages, and so on.

Language is the primary semiotic means we have for encoding ideas and for reinforcing, spreading, and preserving them. As Vico characterized it, language is the *memoria* of a culture, the repository of its meanings. Language allows people to give order and a sense of permanence to the world. When language changes, in fact, so too does the world—one entails the other. No wonder, then, that language has always been felt to constitute the faculty of mind that, more than any other, sets human-kind apart from all other species. The Bible, for instance, starts of with "In the beginning was the Word," in acknowledgment of this belief. In ancient Greece, language and mind were viewed as one and the same, as evidenced by the fact that the Greek term for "speech"—*logos*—designated not only language, but also the reasoning faculty of mind. For the Greeks, it was *logos* that transformed the brute human animal into a reflective thinker.

What is language? Is it a species-specific genetic endowment, developed over many years of adaptive trial and error? Noam Chomsky (chapter 1) has, in fact, claimed that language is a "mental organ" that is present in the brain at birth, equipping humans by the age of two with the ability to develop the specific grammars that cultures require of them. Is he right? Many believe that he is. The linguist Stephen Pinker (1990, 230–231) is one of them:

> A striking discovery of modern generative grammar is that natural languages all seem to be built on the same basic plan. Many differences in basic structure but different settings of a few "parameters" that allow languages to vary, or different choices of rule types from a fairly small inventory of possibilities...On this view, the child only has to set these parameters on the basis of parental input, and the full richness of grammar will ensue when those parametrized rules interact with one another and with universal principles. The parameter-setting view can help explain the universality and rapidity of language acquisition: when the child learns one fact about her language, she can deduce that other facts are also true of it without having to learn them one by one.

There is little doubt that some innate tendencies guide the development of language in human beings. But characterizing them as "mental organs" or "universal grammars" is hardly an adequate characterization of what these are and allow humans to do. Pinker's analysis of language is an acceptable interpretation, among many others, if it is constrained to describing the emergence of grammatical rules in children (see also Pinker 1994, 1997 for elaborate discussions of the innatist view of language). But, then, we would have to define what a grammatical rule is. At that point we would enter into a logical loop of which people such as Chomsky and Pinker are either unaware, or to which they are oblivious. Grammar is what the linguist seeks to describe, namely a series of rules of sentence formation. What are these rules like? They are, apparently, the very rules that the linguist writes. Conclusion—*post hoc ergo propter hoc.*

Upon closer scrutiny, Chomsky's Universal Grammar (UG) theory, as it is called, is hardly a theory of language, but rather the result of a computationist interpretation of language as a device within the mind. This is clearly evident in the choice of the term *language acquisition device* coined by Chomsky to characterize how languages are acquired. But this characterization ignores a much more fundamental creative force in the mind, poetic logic, that is involved not only in the acquisition of language, but also in the development of musical forms, of drawing skills, and of all the other human representational abilities. Since these are also universal and developed during infancy without any training, does the brain therefore also have a "musical mental organ," "a drawing mental organ," and so on? If the role of culture is simply to set the "parameters" that determine the specific kind of grammar that develops in the child, could it not also set, say, the specific melodic parameters that determine the specific forms of musical knowledge that develops in the child? As this analogical argument makes clear, the notions of UG and of language acquisition devices are specious at best and spurious at worst.

Theories of grammar tell us nothing about the ways in which language allows us to deliver the complex *meanings* built into even the simplest of sentences. Despite substantial and noteworthy research on the nature of grammatical rules and syntactic systems since the publication of Chomsky's *Syntactic Structures* in 1957, modern-day grammatical theories seem incapable of adequately explaining the conceptual richness of words put together to form sentences. This is, no doubt, the reason why Chomsky continues to separate grammatical phenomena from meaning (Chomsky 2000, 2002). For Chomsky the crux to understanding language is to unravel the nature of grammatical rules, because, as he claims, the relation words have to each other in sentences is what generates meaning.

Chomsky separates the rules of grammatical systems into two levels, which he calls deep and surface. In the former are the rule-making principles that characterize language as a mental faculty; in the latter are the specific rules that languages develop from the deep structure to produce their particular grammars. Chomsky's main claim is that if we unravel the nature of the rule-making principles in the deep structure, we will have unraveled the nature of the language faculty. In recent writings, he has essentially claimed to have done so by identifying the principle of *recursiveness*, or the repeated application of a rule or procedure to successive results, as the most fundamental and universal type of linguistic rule. By determining the ways in which this principle is converted by different languages into specific surface rules (parameters), we will be able to characterize linguistic diversity as having developed from the same rule-making blueprint.

The idea that all languages are built from the same plan has always been an attractive one. This is perhaps why Chomskyan theory continues to have so many adherents. But what proof is there that the plan is, essentially, nothing more than a set of recursive rule-making principles? Well, there is no proof. It is something that Chomsky deduced by observing syntactic rules in languages such as English. He calls his view of language "X-Bar Theory." If we let, x and y stand for two grammatical categories, and *x-bar* and *y-bar* for the corresponding grammatical phrases, Chomsky claims that rule *x-bar* $x + y$-*bar* is the "DNA" of language. This underlies the generation of all kinds of sentences. Take, as an example, the sentence *The chair is in the corner*. X-Bar Theory would analyze this sentence (schematically at least) as follows:

Deep structure recursion principle:

x-bar $\rightarrow$ x + y-bar

Surface rule:

x-bar = n-bar = noun phrase *(the clock, the corner)*
y-bar = p-bar = prepositional phrase *(in the corner)*

where:

N = noun *(clock, corner)*
p = preposition *(in)*

Structure of *The chair is in the corner*:

n-bar $\rightarrow$ n + p-bar $\rightarrow$ p + n-bar $\rightarrow$ n

Supplemented with an appropriate system of transformational rules that assign word order and sentence relations—e.g., active vs. passive sentences—Chomsky assures us that X-Bar Theory is sufficient to explain the basic blueprint of language. If Chomsky is right, then, the uniqueness of language comes down to a single rule-making principle that specifies how word order develops. But then how would X-Bar Theory explain languages in which word order is virtually irrelevant? Many critics have, in fact, argued that languages such as Classical Latin do not display any evidence of recursiveness, because they encode grammatical relations by means of inflection, i.e., by variations or changes that their words undergo to indicate their relations with other words and changes in meaning. The sentence *The boy loves the girl*, for instance, is rendered in any one of six ways in Latin because the ending on each word informs the speaker or listener what relation it has to the others: (1) *puer* ("boy") is in the nominative case and thus is interpreted by a speaker of Latin as the subject of the sentence; (2) *puellam* ("girl") is in the accusative form (nominative = *puella*) and thus is interpreted as the object of the sentence, no matter where it occurs in it; and (3) *amat* ("loves") is the verb and, like the other parts of speech can occur anywhere in the sentence:

Puer	*amat*	*puellam*	
Puer	*puellam*	*amat*	
Amat	*puer*	*puellam*	"The boy loves the girl"
Amat	*puellam*	*puer*	
Puellam	*amat*	*puer*	
Puellam	*puer*	*amat*	

In English, on the contrary, *The boy loves the girl* and *The girl loves the boy* mean different things. Moreover, other combinations of these words would result in ill-formed sentences: *Loves the boy the girl, Boy the girl the loves,* etc. The only conclusion one can draw from this is that English is a syntactic language, Latin is not. Recursion thus plays an important role in the former, not in the latter. To get around languages such as Latin, Chomsky has claimed that one of the six word combinations above is a "basic" one and the others are its "transformations." But deciding which one is basic is problematic, given that all of the above sentences are perceived as "basic" in Latin according to the context in which each one is uttered: i.e., the choice of one or the other word order depends on stylistic, communicative, and other types of factors, not on syntactic ones.

As it turns out, the deep structure rules (regardless of what they are called in various versions of Chomskyan theory) are really no more than the rules that characterize the syntax of an English declarative sentence. This type of sentence is formed with a *subject*, which is what or who the sentence is about, and a *predicate*, which is what the subject does, thinks, says, etc. or else what is said, thought, indicated, etc. about the subject. The structure of this basic sentence is usually shown by means of a tree diagram:

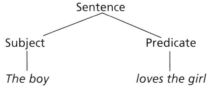

The technique of tree-diagramming is meant to show that sentences are not constructed by a linear concatenation of single words, but rather that the words in them relate to each other hierarchically. This basic plan of the declarative sentence can, of course, be assigned a more detailed characterization. The hierarchical structure of the above sentence *The boy loves the girl* can be shown in more detail as follows (NP = noun phrase, VP = verb phrase, Det = determiner, N = noun, Art = article, Def = definite, V = verb):

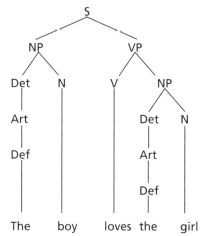

Combinations of the same words that do not fit the hierarchical structure shown by the tree diagram would thus be incomprehensible. This type of analysis purportedly provides a "snapshot" of the internal structure of sentences, thus displaying exactly why we feel that some sentences are genuine, and others are not. However, such snapshots are simply useful procedures for relating the words to each other in terms of grammatical categories; they hardly tell us what generates syntax in the first place. Again, they are examples of *post hoc ergo propter hoc* reasoning.

To explain the relation among types of sentences, Chomsky has proposed the notion of transformational rule, which is purported to show how deep-structure rules are converted into surface-structure strings. Consider, for instance, a sentence such as *Old men and women love that program*. The relevant thing to note about this sentence is that it has potentially two meanings:

1. Old men and women (who are not necessarily old) love that program.
2. Old men and women (who are old as well) love that program.

The source of the ambiguity is traced to the purported fact that two different underlying deep structures come into play—one of which has undergone a transformation. Specifically, (1) is interpreted in one way because it has the deep structure XY + Z, where X = *old*, Y = *men*, and Z = *women*, whereas (2) is interpreted in a different way because it has the deep structure XY + XZ. In the case of (1) no transformational rule has intervened to produce the isomorphic surface string XY + Z; in the case of

(2), however, a transformational rule, akin to factoring in algebra, has intervened to produce the surface string X (Y + Z).

But, then, this solution begs the fundamental question of deciding which sentences are basic and which ones are transformations. It is beyond the scope of the present discussion to deal with the relevant arguments for and against transformational theory. Suffice it to say that the whole edifice of this theory is implanted on the arbitrary view that active affirmative declarative sentences, in their basic outline, reflect the structure of the UG. But this whole line of analysis leads to a host of contradictions and counterinstances that Chomsky has hardly resolved. In the case of the above sentence, transformational theory underplays the fact that the ambiguity can be resolved in nonsyntactic ways, such as in the use of intonation or stress. By stressing *old* and pausing slightly between *old men* and the phrase *and women* one can convey the meaning *old men and women (who are not necessarily old)* in a straightforward nonsyntactic fashion. As Sapir (1921, 87) remarked long before the advent of transformational theory, changing the order of words in a sentence such as *The farmer kills the duckling (Kills the farmer the duckling)*, or omitting any of its words (*Farmer, kill the duckling*) brings about a shift in "modality." Indeed, thirteen distinct meanings could be expressed with the same words by changing order or modifying the words in some way, which reveal more about how these words have been used in a culture's past than they do about some innate grammatical rule system: "The sentence is the outgrowth of historical and of unreasoning psychological forces rather than of a logical synthesis of elements that have been clearly grasped in their individuality." In other words, Sapir contended that sentence structure was reflective of conceptual structure which, in turn, was based on culturally-forged associations of meaning.

The Chomskyan view of linguistic meaning as the product of grammatical structure can, actually, be traced to the ancient world. The Greek scholar Dionysius Thrax, who lived between 170 and 90 BC, wrote what became one of the first models for writing grammars—the *Art of Grammar*. Many later Greek and Latin grammars were based on his model, which was thought to be able to describe all languages. With the spread of Christianity and the translation of the Scriptures into the languages of the new Christians, written literatures began to develop among previously nonliterate peoples. By the late Middle Ages, European scholars generally knew, in addition to their own languages and Latin, the tongues of their nearest neighbors. This set them to thinking about how the grammars of languages might be compared. The revival of Classical learning in the Renaissance, however, led many grammarians to go against the previous grain as they attempted to fit the grammatical facts of different languages into the theoretical framework of Greek and Latin grammar. It was in the sixteenth and seventeenth centuries that this was found to be misguided. The first in-depth surveys of all the then-known languages were undertaken in an attempt to determine which grammatical facts were universal and which were specific to different languages. In the eighteenth century the comparisons became increasingly precise, culminating in the assumption by the German philosopher Leibniz that most languages of Europe, Asia, and Egypt came from the same original language—a language referred to as *Indo-European*.

The English orientalist and jurist Sir William Jones (1746–1794) observed in the same century that Sanskrit bore similarities to Greek and Latin, proposing that the three languages might have developed from a common source. Inspired by Jones, language scholars in the nineteenth century started in earnest to compare languages, discovering that when the sounds of one language corresponded in a regular way to similar sounds in related words in another language, the correspondences were consistent. For example, it was found that the *p-sound* in Latin *pater* ("father") and *ped* ("foot") corresponded regularly to the *f-sound* in English—*father* and *foot*.

It was the Swiss philologist Ferdinand de Saussure (1857–1913) who formalized the view that language grammar was impervious to modification by its use in communication. He referred to the abstract knowledge of grammar as *langue* and to the use of language in communication as *parole*. Saussure used the analogy of a chess game to illustrate the difference between *langue* and *parole*. Chess can be played only by two people who know the rules of the game. This constitutes knowledge of chess *langue*, which includes knowing how to move the pieces on the board, which moves are strategic and which are not, etc.—no matter what size the board, what substance the pieces are made of, and so on. Now, the actual use of this knowledge to play a specific game of chess is *parole*. This involves knowing, essentially, how to apply the rules of chess to respond to certain moves of the opponent.

At first, many linguists rejected the Saussurean dichotomy. Franz Boas (1858–1942), for instance, saw the goal of linguistics as the description of how socially-based communication is organized grammatically (Boas 1940). A grammar, Boas claimed, should describe the relationships of elements in words and sentences to how they are used in actual society and to what they mean to the people who speak the language. But in 1957 Chomsky reestablished the centrality of *langue*, which he renamed *linguistic competence*. His view quickly became the "mainstream" one in linguistics virtually across the world until, in the 1970s, a massive amount of evidence emerged to refute Chomsky's central claim that syntactic rules alone can explain linguistic competence. The first to seriously challenge the Chomskyan paradigm was Dell Hymes (1971), who studied in a detailed fashion how linguistic competence was intertwined with knowledge of how to speak. He called this type of knowledge *communicative competence*. For the sake of historical accuracy, I should mention that many of Hymes's ideas were implicit in the work of precursors such as Sapir (1921), Firth (1957), Austin (1962), and Searle (1969). But it was Hymes who made the study of *parole* a major focus within linguistics. At the core of the notion of communicative competence is the view that verbal structures in discourse are "negotiated" between the interlocutors and that such negotiations influence the actual grammar and vocabulary used (see also Halliday 1973, 1975, 1985 on this point). As Colin Cherry (1957, 9) put it in his monumental study of communication, language among humans "is essentially a social affair."

As discussed in the opening chapter, by the late 1970s research on metaphor came forward to challenge the Chomskyan view even further, leading eventually to the crystallization of a new school of linguistics known as *Cognitive Linguistics* (e.g., Fauconnier 1985, 1997; Deane 1992; Gibbs 1994; Fauconnier and Sweetser 1996; Ungerer and Schmid 1996; Allwood and Gärdenfors 1998; Dirven and Verspoor 1998; Nuyts 2001; Lee 2001; Leezenberg 2001; Fauconnier and Turner 2002). The main figure in the Cognitive Linguistic movement is the American linguist Ronald Langacker (e.g., 1987, 1990, 1999), who has shown repeatedly how concepts, not syntactic rules, influence language competence. The movement is not, however, without historical antecedents. The philosopher Johann Gottfried von Herder (1744–1803), for instance, claimed that there was an implicit connection between grammar and what he called "ethnic character" (Herder 1784). Subsequently, Wilhelm von Humboldt (1767–1835) gave Herder's hypothesis a more empirical formulation when he provided a detailed examination of the structures of language as conveyors of the thought and behavior patterns of the people using it for communication (Humboldt 1836). And, as mentioned at the start of this chapter, Sapir and Whorf wanted to make the study of the relation between language and thought the central feature of linguistic science. They foreshadowed the Cognitive Linguistic movement by claiming that human ideas, concepts, feelings, and characteristic social behaviors are mirrored in the categories that specific languages employ to codify them. As Whorf (1956, 153) eloquently put it: "The world is presented in a kaleidoscopic flux of impressions which has to be organized by our minds—and this means largely by the linguistic systems in our minds." Cognitive Linguistics is, in effect, an attempt to make good on the Sapir-Whorf agenda for linguistic science. The fundamental principle espoused by it is that language structures cannot be studied separately from human emotions, ideas, and social traditions.

Conceptual Metaphors

The Cognitive Linguistic movement is, as mentioned, propelled by the notion of conceptual metaphor (e.g., Casad 1996; Palmer 1996; Yu 1998; Barcelona 1999; Cameron and Low 1999; Lee 2001). Recall that a conceptual metaphor is, essentially, a thought formula that crystallizes from the linkage of a target and a source domain. The mental feature that guides the linkage of the two domains is, as argued in the previous chapter, sense implication. For example, the physical sense of "up and down" guides the conceptualization of a host of ideas and beliefs that are felt to implicate this sense in some imaginary way (see also Kinder 1991):

3.	*happiness is up*	=	I'm feeling *up* today.
4.	*sadness is down*	=	She's feeling *down* today.
5.	*more is up*	=	My income *went up* last year.
6.	*less is down*	=	Her salary *went down* this year.

Now, the formation of a conceptual metaphor through associative thinking does not stop at language. It also informs representational practices in general. To see how this is so, consider the concept of *time* in English. Common metaphorical portrayals of this concept are as a *journey (There's a long way to go yet)*, as a *substance (There's not enough time left)*, as a *person (Time comes and goes)* and as a *device (Time keeps ticking on)*. These source domains manifest themselves as representations such as mythical figures that reify *time is a person*, such as *Father Time*, narratives that instantiate *time is a device*, such as *The Time Machine* (1895) by H. G. Wells (1866–1946), and so on. But that is not all that such conceptual metaphors do. They also provide psychological insight into how our concepts of time came about in the first place and how they have changed. The earliest type of timekeeping device, dating back to 3500 BC, was the *gnomon* (shadow clock), a vertical stick or shaft that casts a shadow. Methods of measuring hours in the absence of sunlight included the notched candle and the Chinese practice of burning a knotted rope. Other ancient devices included the hourglass and the water clock, in which the flow of water indicated the passage of time. The first recorded examples of the mechanical clock come from the fourteenth century—a device that *ipso facto* changed the world, leading to a new conceptualization of *time* as something that could be measured and thus anticipated exactly. In English-speaking cultures this has had a truly profound effect on the meaning of time. It has led, for instance, to the use of two words to refer to timekeeping devices—*clock* and *watch*. It is called *watch* if the device is portable and can be worn on the human body, usually on the wrist, but *clock* if it is to be put somewhere, for example, on a table or on a wall. In Italian, on the other hand, no such conceptual distinction has been encoded lexically. The word *orologio* refers to any device for keeping track of time, with no regard to its "portability:"

Italian	orologio	
English	watch (portable)	clock (nonportable)
Concept	device for keeping time	

This does not mean that Italians do not have the linguistic resources for making the distinction, if needed. Indeed, the phrase *da + place* allows speakers to provide exactly this kind of information:

orologio da polso	=	wrist watch
orologio da tavolo	=	table clock
orologio da muro	=	wall clock

Italians do not find it necessary to distinguish conceptually between *watches* and *clocks* as a necessary fact of life. They can refer to the portability of the device in other ways, if the situation requires them to do so. Speakers of English, on the other hand, think of the portability distinction as a necessary fact of life, attending to it on a regular basis, as forced to do so by the two words at their disposal. Historically speaking, the word *watch* originated in the 1850s when people started strapping clocks around their wrists. As the psychologist Robert Levine (1997) argues, this introduced a cultural fixation with watching time pass that has been incorporated into English vocabulary.

The notion of conceptual metaphor has far-reaching implications for studying the language-culture interface. The work in CMT has come forward, in effect, to show how conceptual metaphors coalesce into a system of cultural meanings that inform representations, symbols, rituals, activities, and behaviors (Dundes 1972; Kövecses 1986, 1988, 1990). Lakoff and Johnson (1980) call the coalescence of meanings *idealized cognitive/cultural models* (ICMs). These are defined as over-arching models that result from the repeated association of certain target domains with specific kinds of source domains. To see what this means, consider the target domain of *ideas*. The following conceptual metaphors, among others, are used in English to deliver the meaning of this concept:

ideas are food

7. Those ideas left a *sour taste* in my mouth.
8. It's hard to *digest* all those ideas at once.
9. Even though he is a *voracious* reader; he can't *chew* all those ideas.
10. That teacher is always *spoon-feeding* her students.

ideas are persons

11. Darwin is the *father* of modern biology.
12. Those medieval ideas continue to *live on* even today.
13. Cognitive linguistics is still in its *infancy.*
14. Maybe we should *resurrect* that ancient idea.
15. She *breathed* new life into that old idea.

ideas are fashion

16. That idea went out of *style* several years ago.
17. Those scientists are the *avant-garde* of their field.
18. Counterculture ideas are no longer in *vogue.*
19. The field of semiotics has become truly *chic.*
20. That idea is an old *hat.*

ideas are buildings

21. That idea is planted on *solid ground.*
22. That is a *cornerstone* idea of modern-day biology.
23. That is only a *framework* for a new theory.
24. That theory is starting to *crumble* under the weight of criticism.

ideas are plants

25. That idea has many *ramifications.*
26. How many *branches* of knowledge are there?
27. That theory has deep historical *roots.*
28. That idea has produced many *offshoots.*

ideas are commodities

29. That idea is *worthless.*
30. You must *package* your ideas more attractively.
31. You'll be able to *sell* your ideas easily.

ideas are geometrical figures

32. That idea is rather *square.*
33. His ideas are *parallel* to mine.
34. His ideas are *diametrically opposite* to mine.
35. What's the *point* of your idea?

ideas can be seen

36. I don't *see* what that idea is about.
37. I can't quite *visualize* what you mean by that idea.
38. Let me take a *look* at that theory.

Now, the constant juxtaposition of such source domains in common discourse produces, cumulatively, an ICM of *ideas*, i.e., an array of source domains that can be accessed separately, in tandem, or alternatively to discuss ideas of various kinds, and to represent them in different but interconnected ways. So, for example, a sentence such as *I see that your idea has many ramifications, given that it is on solid ground* has been constructed by enlisting three of the above source domains that make up the ICM of *ideas* (*seeing, plants, buildings*). The associative structure of an ICM can be shown as follows:

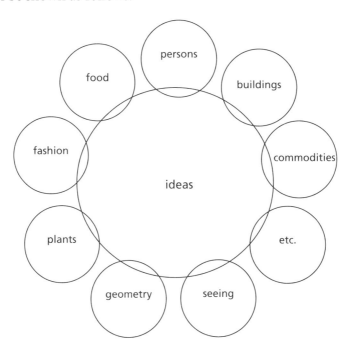

I referred to the formation of an ICM as a *layering* process in the previous chapter. The higher the "density" of layering, i.e., the greater the number of source domains that constitute an ICM, the more productive the concept. *Productivity* can thus be defined as the number of layers (different source domains) utilized to produce an ICM. Incidentally, it would appear that some of the source domains used to produce a specific type of concept seem to be universal, while others seem to be culture-specific. For example, a conceptual metaphor such as *ideas can be seen from above* is relatively understandable across cultures: i.e., people from non-English-speaking cultures could easily figure out what the statements that instantiate this conceptual metaphor mean if they were translated to them, because *vision* appears to be used universally to implicate *ideas*. The *ideas are geometrical figures* conceptual metaphor, on the other hand, is more likely to be understood in culture-specific ways or only in cultures where Euclidean geometry is part of their traditions. The statements that instantiate it are thus much less likely to be understood when translated.

Work in CMT has made it possible to evaluate the productivity of concepts cross-culturally and to identify any universals that may exist in conceptualization. As mentioned, from the relevant research, it would seem that conceptual metaphors involving *vision*, *seeing*, and *light* are common cross-cultural ones for referring to intellectual qualities and processes. The number of constructions (words, idioms, phrases, etc.) that they produce in vocabularies across the world is immeasurable. Here is a handful of words constructed to implicate vision in English:

39. *flash* of insight
40. *spark* of genius
41. a *bright* mind
42. a *brilliant* idea
43. a *flicker* of intelligence
44. a *luminous* achievement
45. a *shining* mind
46. a *bright* fire in his eyes
47. *sparking* interest in a subject
48. words *glowing* with meaning
49. *flickering* ideas

Actually, the use of vision is only one of the sense-based source domains utilized in the delivery of mentation concepts. Touch, hearing, taste, and smell, too, have been found cross-culturally as other source domains, albeit with a lower productivity *(He touched upon a new idea, I hear what your are trying to say to me, That idea leaves a bad taste in one's mouth, I can smell a new idea)*. Sensory source domains lie at the root of many mentation concepts in English (Sweetser 1990):

50. *perceive* (from Latin *-cipio* "to seize")
51. *scrutinize* (from Latin *scrutari* "to pick through trash")
52. *examine* (from Latin *ex* + *agmen-* "to pull out from a row")
53. *discern* (from Latin *dis* + *cerno* "to separate")
54. *prospect* (from Latin *pro* + *spectus* "looking ahead")
55. *speculate* (from Latin *speculari* "to look at")
56. *comprehend* (from Latin *prehendere* "to grasp")
57. *idea* (from Greek *ideein* "to see")
58. *theory* (from Greek *theoria* "view")
59. *think* (from Old English *thincean* "to take, handle")
60. *understand* (from Old English *ongietan* "to see, hear, feel")
61. *apprehend* (from Latin "to seize, lay hold of")

A cursory glance at various unrelated languages suggests a similar etymological tendency:

62. Hebrew *litpos* "to grasp" means "to understand."
63. Maori *kura* "seeing" refers to "knowledge in general;" and *kia marama te titiro* "to see clearly" to "understanding."
64. Japanese *yoin* "reverberating sound" designates "human feelings."
65. Chinese *takuan* "to have seen through life" refers to the ability "to understand that some things cannot be understood."
66. Sanskrit *maya* "to measure with the eye" refers to the danger inherent in relying upon one's mind to visualize the world.

Not all words for mentation are, of course, constructed on the basis of sensory source domains. The word *contemplate*, for instance, derives from Latin *templum* "temple"—the temple being the place where one "contemplates." And the word *mind* has referred exclusively to abstract mentation for at least 5,000 years (Wescott 1978, 27). But by and large, sensory source domains seem to dominate in this area of concept-formation in languages across the world. The resulting metaphors are known as "root" metaphors. They are no longer recognized as implicating sensory processes, because they have become conventionalized through protracted usage. Edie (1976, 165) offers the following relevant observation:

> A word which primarily designates a perceptual phenomenon —for example the perception of light—once constituted is available *for a new purpose* and can be used with a new intention —for example to denote the process of intellectual understanding, and we speak of (mental) illumination. Once established, the metaphorical use of the original word is no longer noticed; its essential ambiguity tends to fall below the level of awareness from the moment that it is taken as designating another, now distinguishable, experience.

Another seemingly universal tendency in concept-formation is the use of the *body* as a source domain to name things. Take, for instance, the perception that the automobile is a body and thus as a protective shell of the Self. In the public world of traffic, it is perceived as creating a space around the physical body, which is as inviolable as the body itself. Any transgression against the car body is felt *ipso facto* to be a transgression against the person driving the car. This is why we name some of the automobile's parts as if they were body parts—e.g., "head lights," "rear end." In the Western Apache language of east-central Arizona this metaphorical naming process has been extended to the entire automobile (Basso 1990, 15–24): e.g., the hood is called a "nose," the headlights "eyes," the windshield "forehead," the area from the top of the windshield to the front bumper "face," the front wheels "hands and arms," the rear wheels "feet," the items under the hood "innards," the battery "liver," the electrical wiring "veins," the gas tank "stomach," the distributor "heart," the radiator "lung," and the radiator hoses "intestines."

The use of the body as a source domain extends to the naming of many and varied referents. Here are a few examples in English:

67. a *body* of water
68. the *body* of a work
69. a *body* of people
70. the *head* of the household
71. the *head* of a table
72. the *head* of an organization
73. the *face* of a clock
74. the *foot* of a mountain
75. the *leg* of a race
76. the *eye* of the needle
77. the *eye* of a storm

Known as anthropomorphism, it is a phenomenon that reveals clearly how sense implication works in producing our "models" of the world. This is why we say that cups have *lips*, combs *teeth*, fixtures *knuckles* and *joints*, texts *footnotes* and *appendixes*, and so on. We also extend the body into the domain of human activities themselves, as if they too were products of bodily processes. This is why we say such things as:

78. *holding* a meeting
79. taking things at *face* value
80. *nosing* around
81. *mouthing* lyrics
82. *shouldering* a burden
83. *knuckling* under
84. going *belly up*
85. *toeing* the line

Across the world, societies too tend to be perceived as *communal bodies*. This is why they are described in bodily terms—as being *healthy, sick, vibrant, beautiful, ugly, neat, dirty, organized, disorganized,* and so on. Anthropomorphism is a basic mode of conceptualizing. This is why in early myths and in the stories we tell children personification is so typical. Expressions such as *The storm raged all night long* and *The dark clouds told me a storm was coming* are residues of this anthropomorphic mythological tendency. And this is why Nature itself is perceived to be a fertile mother figure which produces *knowledge* in the form of *branches* growing from *trees* and *ideas* in the form of *plants* with *offshoots, roots,* and the like.

In sum, CMT has shown that language cannot be studied independently from culture and thought, as Sapir and Whorf, and Vico before them correctly pointed out. In every word, phrase, or sentence is a conceptualization of the world that is likely born of metaphor. The study of metaphor thus brings the "conceptualization out in the open," so to speak, so that we can once again recapture the poetic logic behind it.

Conceptual Metonyms

As mentioned in the opening chapter, the practice in CMT is to use the term *metaphor* to encompass various kinds of tropes. Within this new paradigm anthropomorphism would be seen as a specific type of conceptual metaphor, in which the target domain involves an animal or inanimate object and the source domain implicates traits that are associated with human beings:

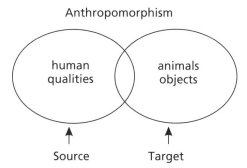

However, two tropes that are considered to be cognitively different from metaphor are *metonymy* (and its converse *synecdoche)* and *irony*. The latter will be discussed in the next section. Metonymy is the referential process by which the name of one thing is used in place of that of another associated with it or suggested by it (e.g., the *White House* for the *President*). Conceptually, it can be defined as the process of using a part of a domain to represent the whole domain, or aspects of a domain to implicate either the whole domain or subsections of it:

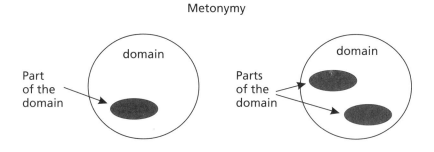

The first process is known more precisely as synecdoche. But only the term metonymy will be used in this book, as is the practice generally in CMT, perhaps because, as Kennedy (1999, 90) aptly puts it, metonymy is psychologically more general than synecdoche: "We can show a part to suggest the whole, but we can also show something, like a bullseye target, that is not actually a part of the whole" (see also Panther and Radden 1999 on this distinction).

Like metaphor, metonymy is ever-present in common everyday discourse. Here are some of its instantiations in English (Lakoff and Johnson 1980, 35–40):

86. She likes to read *Dostoyevski* (= the writings of Dostoyevski).
87. He's in *dance* (= the dancing profession).
88. My mom frowns on *nose rings* (= the wearing of nose rings).
89. Only new *windshield wipers* will satisfy him (= having new wipers).
90. The *automobile* is destroying our health (= the collection of automobiles).
91. We need a couple of *strong bodies* for our teams (= strong people).
92. I've got a new *set of wheels* (= car).
93. We need *new blood* in this organization (= new people).

In parallelism with the notion of conceptual metaphor, the term *conceptual metonym* can be used to refer to concepts forged metonymically. So, for example, the use of the *face* to represent the entire *person* can be seen to constitute a particular type of metonymic formula—*the face is the person*:

94. He's just another pretty *face*.
95. There are an awful lot of *faces* in the audience.
96. We need some new *faces* around here.
97. You must put on a brave *face*.

Like conceptual metaphors, conceptual metonyms surface constantly in all kinds of situations and speech acts, revealing however a more culture-specific form of poetic logic:

a body part for the person

98. Get your *butt* over here!
99. The Milwaukee Brewers need a *stronger arm* in right field.
100. We don't hire *beards* around here.

the producer (brand) for the product

101. I'll have a *Heineken* instead of a *Budweiser*.
102. We bought a *Ford*, as we always do.

103. He's got a fake *Rembrandt* in his office.

the object used for the user
104. My *piano* is sick today.
105. The *meat and potatoes* is a lousy tipper.
106. The *buses* are on strike.

the person, place, or object for the event
107. *Napoleon* lost at Waterloo.
108. *Montreal* won a lot of Stanley Cups.
109. A Mercedes rear-ended *me*.

the institution or place for the people responsible
110. *Shell* has raised its prices again.
111. The *Church* thinks that promiscuity is immoral.
112. I don't approve of *Washington's* actions.

the place for the institution
113. The *White House* isn't saying anything.
114. *Milan* is introducing new jackets this year.
115. *Wall Street* is in a panic.

Unlike metaphor, metonymy does not function to create knowledge through associative reasoning, but rather it allows people to cast specific kinds of light on certain situations, so as to be able to make some social or personal comment on them. In (98), for instance, the use of *butt* to stand for a *person* forces us to focus on a part of human anatomy, the buttocks, that elicits images of laziness and indolence, given that the butt is the anatomical part used for sitting. In (106), the choice of *buses* to stand for those who drive them forces us to evaluate the consequences of the strike—by stopping buses the strikers have inconvenienced everyone. Metonymy is not productive of new knowledge. It is designed to allow people to provide perspective, opinion, point of view, or criticism.

However, this does not mean that conceptual metonyms do not play a significant role in shaping the meaning pathways in the network of culture. The *face is the person* conceptual metonym, for example, is interconnected to the practice of portraiture, which focuses on the face as a metonym of personality and character. And the conceptual metonym *a body part stands for the sexual person* is, of course, the source of the psychocultural phenomenon referred to as *fetishism*. Originally, fetishes were inanimate objects that were thought to have supernatural attributes. In tribal cultures, the fetish is typically a figure modeled or carved from clay, stone, wood, or some other material, resembling a deified animal or some sacred thing. Sometimes it is the animal itself, or a tree, river, rock, or place associated with it. In some tribes, belief in the powers of the fetish is so strong that fetishism develops into idolatry. This is an extreme form of *animism*—the belief that spirits either inhabit or communicate with humans through material objects.

Animism is not limited to tribal or premodern cultures. On the contrary, it is alive and well even in modern-day Western cultures, whether or not the people who live in them realize it. In addition to the fetishes that incite sexual urges or fantasies in some people—feet, shoes, intimate female apparel—there are many metonymic symbols in our culture that can only be explained in animism terms. In the 1970s, for example, there emerged a craze in American society for "pet rocks." Many social critics considered this fad simply a quick way to make money, foisted upon a gullible public spoiled by consumerism. But, in my view, it was more of an indulgence in animism than anything else. Unconscious animism also manifests itself in the common view that some objects are magical. This is why, if they are lost, impending danger is feared to ensue. If, however, they are found serendipitously—as for instance when one finds a "lucky penny"—then it is believed that the gods or Fortune will look auspiciously upon the finder.

Conceptual Eireins

Irony constitutes a contrasting strategy in which words are used to convey a meaning contrary to their literal sense. Irony thus creates a discrepancy between words and their meanings. To put it more specifically, ironic concepts are formed by associating target domains (e.g., *torture, torment,* etc.) with incongruous source domains (*love, enjoyment,* etc.):

116. You *love* being *tortured*, don't you?

117. She *loves* getting *hurt.*

118. He *enjoys torment.*

These are, in effect, instantiations of a thought formula that can be shown as follows: *pain is understood by contrasting it to pleasure.* In irony, the context is critical since without it such statements would be interpreted literally. If the person alluded to was a masochist, then the statements would hardly be construed as ironic. For them to be interpreted as ironic, the person must be in real torment and dislike it. For the sake of terminological consistency, an ironic concept can be called a *conceptual eirein* (*eirein* is the Greek word from which our term *irony* is derived), in analogy to conceptual metaphor and conceptual metonym.

Conceptual eireins have various cognitive functions (Hutcheon 1995; Barbe 1995). They are used to strengthen a statement by forcing the listener or reader to seek its true meaning. Suppose, for example, that a ballet dancer trips several times and her choreographer says, "You were very graceful!" The choreographer is using irony so that the dancer will become aware that he or she knows of the trips and that something has to be done about them. Another function of irony is to relay to an interlocutor something that others do not know. In the Greek tragedy *Oedipus Rex* by Sophocles, for instance, Oedipus kills a man (chapter 1). He does not know that the man is Laius, his father. Oedipus puts a curse on the slayer of Laius. The irony is that Oedipus has unknowingly cursed himself. Irony is also used to highlight events that work out contrary to expectations. Suppose that a home town is preparing a party for a returning soldier. But the soldier is killed in an accident on his way home. The irony comes from the contrast between the expectations of the people and the actual situation.

Irony is particularly productive in humor, satire, and parody. Irony turns conceptual metaphors on their head, so to speak, to produce the humorous, satirical, or parodic perspective. For example, in adolescent slang the *people are animals* conceptual metaphor is used to create such ironic forms as *megabitch, party animal, dog* (unattractive person), *wimp dog* (male with little personality), among others. The *body is the person* conceptual metaphor is the ironic basis for expressions such as *M.L.A. = massive lip action* (passionate kissing), *barf* (vomit), *blimp boat* (obese person), etc. (Danesi 2003).

It is interesting to note that irony emerges relatively late in verbal development (Winner 1988). It appears as a linguistic strategy around puberty. At that point, language becomes a powerful weapon in social interaction, used for criticizing human habits, ideas, and vacuous rituals. But the ironic intellect is a short-lived one. Like adolescence, it fades quickly. The proof of this can be found in a simple observation—works of metaphor (such as the great poetry of Dante) remain and are appreciated; works of pure irony, such as those of Voltaire, seem to lose their impact over time, unless, of course, the culture that adopts them is plagued by the same kinds of inanities satirized by them.

Grammar

In addition to providing insights the metaphorical origin and usage of words, the work in CMT has also provided a perspective on how metaphorical thinking may shape the very structure of grammar (Cienki, Luka, and Smith 2001). The gist of the relevant research can be summarized with the notion of *reflexivization*, i.e., with the idea that the form and dispersion of words in sentences are "reflexive" of conceptual structure. Reflexivization can be seen, for instance, in the selection of a part of speech (Sebeok and Danesi 2000). Consider the use of *snake* as an instantiation of the conceptual metaphor *people are animals*. In specific sentences, it can show up as a verb (119), if it is the snake's movements that are implicated, or as an adjective (120), if it is a quality of the snake that is implicated instead:

119. The professor *snaked* his way around the issue.
120. The professor has a *snaky* way of doing things.

The reflexivization of *snake* in (119) emphasizes the movement of snakes in the portrayal of personality, while in (120) it is a serpentine quality of character that is intended. The two different grammatical categories can be seen to *reflect* different nuances in meaning.

Differences in word order, too, can often be traced to conceptual distinctions. In Italian, for instance, the difference between the literal and metaphorical meaning of an adjectival concept is sometimes reflected by the different position of the adjective in a noun phrase:

121. Lui è un uomo *povero* ("He's an indigent man").
122. Lui è un *povero* uomo ("He's a forlorn man").

In (121) it is the literal meaning of *povero* that is reflected in the noun phrase by the post-positioning of the adjective with respect to the noun. In (122) the metaphorical meaning of *povero* is brought out by means of its pre-positioning with respect to the noun, alerting the interlocutor in an anticipatory fashion to this meaning.

As another example of how concepts are reflexivized grammatically, consider the use of the English prepositions *since* and *for* in sentences such as the following:

123. I have been living here *since* 2000.

124. I have known Lucy *since* August.

125. I have not been able to sleep *since* Monday.

126. I have been living here *for* twenty years.

127. I have known Lucy *for* nine months.

128. I have not been able to sleep *for* seven days.

The complements that follow *since* are vehicles that reflexivize *points in time*, i.e., they are complements that reflexivize the metaphorical conceptualization of *time* as *a point on a timeline* on which specific years, months, etc. can be shown: *2000, August, Monday,* etc.

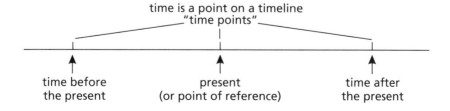

Complements that follow *for*, on the other hand, reflexivize a metaphorical conceptualization of *time* as *a quantity*: i.e., *twenty years*, *nine months*, *seven days*, etc. Simply put, complements introduced by *since* are reflexes of the conceptual metaphor *time is a point on a timeline*; those introduced by *for* are reflexes of *time is a quantity*. The use of *since* or *for* is obviously intended to signal this conceptual difference.

Sometimes it is the image schema underlying a conceptual metaphor that shapes sentence structure or lexical selection. Take, as case-in-point, the use of the verbs *fare* "to make," *essere* "to be," and *avere* "to have" in Italian when the adjectives *caldo* "hot" and *freddo* "cold" refer to weather, things, or people:

- The verb *fare* is used when they refer to the weather—*fa caldo* (literally) "it makes hot," *fa freddo* (literally) "it makes cold."
- The verb *essere* is used when they refer to objects—*è caldo* "it is hot," *è freddo* "it is cold."
- The verb *avere* is used when they refer to people—*ha caldo* "he or she is hot," *ha freddo* "he or she is cold."

Evidently, the use of one verb or the other is motivated by the [container] image schema. If the [container] is the environment, then the *caldo* or *freddo* is "made" by Nature *(fa caldo/freddo)*; if it is the human body, then the body "has" the heat or cold inside it *(ha caldo/freddo)*; and if it is an object, then the object "is" itself hot or cold *(è caldo/freddo)*. It is interesting to note, parenthetically, that there are a host of concepts in Italian that are reflexivized in this way. For example, "rightness" and "sleepiness" are also conceptualized as "contained" substances. This is why "I am right" and "I am sleepy" are rendered in Italian as *ho ragione* ("I have rightness") and *ho sonno* ("I have sleepiness"). To put it in psychological terms, grammar appears to be a code that gives form to the sense implication process.

The evidence to support reflexivization comes primarily from the work in Cognitive Linguistics. Ronald Langacker (e.g., 1987, 1990, 1999), one of the founders of the movement, has even argued that the parts of speech themselves originated through what has been called sense implication in this book. Nouns, for instance, encode the image schema of a [region] in mind-space. A count noun such as *leaf* is envisioned as referring to something that encircles a [bounded region], and a mass noun such as *water* a [nonbounded region]. Now, this difference in image schematic structure induces grammatical distinctions. Thus, because [bounded] referents can be counted, the form *leaf* has a corresponding plural form *leaves*, but *water* does not (unless it is used metaphorically as in *the waters of Babylon*). Moreover *leaf* can be preceded by an indefinite article *(a leaf)*, *water* cannot.

Consider, as another example of reflexivization, the relation be-tween an active and a passive sentence such as *Alexander ate the apple* vs. *The apple was eaten by Alexander.* In Chomskyan linguistics, the former is considered the basic (deep structure) string and the latter a surface struc-ture string that results from the application of a transformational rule. But this type of analysis tells us nothing about the conceptual contrast that the two sentences reflect. In the active sentence, the subject (*Alexan-der*) is in the foreground of the mind's eye, while the object (*apple*) is in the background. The action implicated by the verb (*eating*) is spotlighted as an activity of the subject. The overall mental image schema that the active sentence conveys is, therefore, one of the subject as a [perpetrator] of an action. The passive sentence, on the other hand, implicates a differ-ence in the position of the foreground and the background in the mind's eye. It brings the *apple* to the foreground, relegating the eater, *Alexander*, to the background. The action of eating is now spotlighted on the object, or the [receiver] of the action. The conceptual shift between [perpetrator] and [receiver] is, clearly, built into the structure of each type of sentence. Passive sentences are hardly just surface structure variants of deep struc-ture active ones. They encode, in actual fact, a different mental angle from which to see the same action conceptually.

It is worth noting that, even before the advent of Cognitive Linguis-tics, the philosopher Ludwig Wittgenstein (1889–1951) had character-ized sentences as structures designed to represent features of the world in the same way that pictures do (Wittgenstein 1921). The lines and shapes of drawings show how things are related to each other; so too, he claimed, do the ways in which words are put together in sentences. A half century later, the psychologist Rudolf Arnheim (1969, 242) pre-sented a similar pictorial account of sentences, explaining the *raison d'être* of function words such as prepositions and conjunctions as fol-lows:

> I referred in an earlier chapter to the barrier character of "but," quite different from "although," which does not stop the flow of action but merely burdens it with a complication. Causal re-lations...are directly perceivable actions; therefore "because" introduces an effectuating agent, which pushes things along. How different is the victorious overcoming of a hurdle con-jured up by "in spite of" from the displacement in "either-or" or "instead;" and how different is the stable attachment of "with" or "of" from the belligerent "against."

Reflexivization manifests itself at all levels of language structure. It can even be used to explain a phonetic phenomenon known as *sound symbolism*. This is the tendency to perceive the sounds in words as re-flecting some property of their referents. For example, people tend to perceive certain vowels, such as the *i-vowel* in *chin*, as "light" and others, such as the *u-vowel* in *chunk*, as "heavy." In one relevant study, the psycholinguist Roger Brown (1970, 258–273) asked native speakers of English to listen to pairs of antonyms from a language unrelated to English and then to try to guess, given the English equivalents, which foreign word translated which English word by attending to their sounds. When he asked them, for example, to match the words *ch'ing* and *chung* to the English equivalents *light* and *heavy*, Brown found that about 90% of English speakers correctly matched *ch'ing* to *light* and *chung* to *heavy*. He concluded that the degree of translation accuracy could only be explained "as indicative of a primitive phonetic symbolism deriving from the origin of speech in some kind of imitative or physiognomic linkage of sounds and meanings" (Brown 1970, 272). To put it slightly differently, it would seem that people perceive words constructed with *i-vowels* as referring to things that have a "lightness" quality to them and those constructed with *u-vowels* as referring to things that have a 'heaviness" quality to them.

Sound symbolism theory was pioneered by Morris Swadesh (1951, 1959, 1971). Swadesh drew attention to such suggestive features as the fact that many of the world's languages used *i-vowels* to express [nearness] concepts and *a-vowels* and *u-vowels* to express [distance] concepts. Such coincidences suggested to him that [nearness] is probably built into the phonics of a word by its construction with *i-vowels* because it is implicated in the relative nearness of the lips in the articulation of *i-vowels*; while the complementary notion of [distance] is implicated by the relative openness of the lips in the pronunciation of *a-vowels* and *u-vowels*:

Nearness Concepts	*Distance Concepts*
here = [hiːr]	there= [ðæːr]
near = [niːr]	far= [faːr]
this = [ðíːs]	that= [ðaeːt]
etc.	etc.

It is beyond the purpose here to discuss the relevant research findings on sound symbolism in the world's languages (see, for instance, Hinton, Nichols, and Ohala 1994). Suffice it to say that it is a widespread phenomenon, guiding the early development of language and manifesting itself across cultures in such common ways as follows:

- *alliteration*, or the repetition of sounds for various effects: *sing-song; no-no*;
- the *lengthening* of sounds for emphasis: *Yesssss!, Noooooo!*;

- the use of *intonation* to express emotional states, to emphasize, to shock, etc.: *Are you absolutely sure? Noooooo way!*;
- *sound-modeling*, as in the language of cartoons and comic books: *Zap!, Boom!, Pow!*;
- *onomatopoeic* descriptions of people and things: a snake is described as *slithery, slippery, sneaky*, etc.;
- *loudness* to convey a state of anger; an increased *rate of speech* urgency; *whispering* conspiracy; etc.

It is relevant to note that Vico's account of the origin of grammar largely prefigured sound symbolism theory. He suggested that the first words of humanity were formed onomatopoeically, a tendency "which we still find in children happily expressing themselves" (Bergin and Fisch 1984, 447). Then came interjections, "which are sounds articulated under the impetus of violent passions" (Bergin and Fisch 1984, 448). Pronouns followed because they made it possible to communicate "ideas with others concerning things which we cannot name or whose names another may not understand" (Bergin and Fisch 1984, 450). Particles, nouns, and verbs respectively complete the formation of grammar:

> Last of all, the authors of the languages formed the verbs, as we observe children expressing nouns and particles but leaving the verbs to be understood. For nouns awaken ideas which leave firm traces; particles signifying modifications, do the same; but verbs signify motions, which involve past and future, which are measured from the indivisible present. (Bergin and Fisch 1984, 453)

The presence of sound symbolism and other sense implication phenomena in the formation of words, phrases, and sentences suggests that language *form* mirrors in some way the *content* it encodes. In this theoretical framework, language can be defined as a sign system for creating forms that implicate the sensory, emotional, and affective properties perceived in the referents they encode.

Chapter 4

CULTURE

Culture is the name for what people
are interested in, their thoughts, their
models, the books they read and the
speeches they hear, their table-talk,
gossip, controversies, historical sense
and scientific training, the values they
appreciate, the quality of life they admire.
All communities have a culture. It is the
climate of their civilization.
— Walter Lippmann (1889–1974)

The need to unravel a purpose to reality is the driving force behind humanity's most luminous evolutionary accomplishment, *culture*, the system of meanings that reflect how we give expression to this need. As argued throughout this book, such expression cannot help but be shaped fundamentally by metaphorical reasoning, given the "poetic" nature of the human brain. The objective of this chapter is to take a closer look at the metaphorical origins and constitution of culture. It was, in fact, one of Vico's greatest insights to suggest that culture is a product of poetic logic; namely, a system of expressive and representational practices that we have culled from the many and varied sense implications we make as we search for purpose to reality. The Vichian perspective of culture would also explain why cultures are in constant flux. Poetic logic is an imaginative force within the human brain that is constantly impelling it to seek out new ways to make sense of things, as it attempts to unravel the nature of reality.

The *raison d'être* of philosophy has always been to determine whether or not reality can exist independently from the cultures human beings create to think about it. Is everything "out there," philosophers ask, something to be figured out, like a puzzle? Or is reality no more than a figment of the human imagination that varies as cultures vary? Although an answer to this question will clearly never be possible, we can certainly gain great insight into the nature of reality by examining how we go about literally "imagining" it as cultural collectivities. As Vico aptly put it, "when we wish to give utterance to our understanding of spiritual things, we must seek aid from our imagination to explain them and, like painters, form human images of them" (Bergin and Fisch 1984, 402). As the historian of science Jacob Bronowski (1977, 24) also observed, centuries later, to imagine what reality is all about "means to make images and to move them about inside one's head in new arrangements."

Cultural Groupthink

Culture includes the arts, beliefs, customs, institutions, inventions, language, symbols, rituals, technology, and values produced and shared by a group of people tied together by the forces of history. For this reason, a culture produces similar behavior and thinking habits among the members of the group. The process by which such so-called "groupthink" develops is called *enculturation*.

The formation of groupthink is shaped in large part by the constant layering of conceptual metaphors in discourse. The notion of Idealized Cognitive Model (ICM), which was introduced in the previous chapter, is thus a useful one for investigating groupthink. ICMs crystallize from layers of source domains that are designed to provide different perspectives of the same concept or target domain. The structure of an ICM can thus be represented with one large circle (the target domain) around which smaller circles (the source domains) appear to cluster (T = target domain, S = source domain):

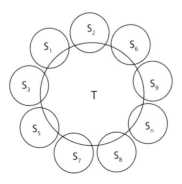

The process involved in the formation of this kind ICM can thus be called *clustering*. The ICM of *ideas*, as we saw in the previous chapter, is formed in this way—namely, through the clustering of source domains such as *food, plants, geometry*, and so on.

Another feature of groupthink consists in the use of the same source domain to deliver a series of different target concepts. This process can be called *radiation*, since it can be envisioned as a single source domain "radiating outwards" to deliver different target domains. For example, the *plant* source domain above not only allows us to conceptualize ideas *(That idea has deep ramifications)*, but also such other abstract concepts as love *(Our love has deep roots)*, influence *(His influence is sprouting all over)*, success *(His career has borne great fruit)*, knowledge *(That discipline has many branches)*, wisdom *(His wisdom has deep roots)*, and friendship *(Their friendship is starting to bud just now)*, among many others. The radiation structure of *plants* can be shown as follows (T = target domain, S = source domain):

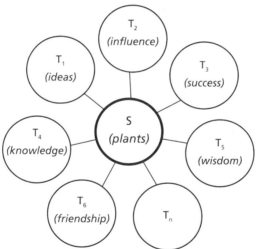

Clustering and radiation are features of groupthink that allow us to pinpoint the reasons why certain concepts are felt to be connected, and in which ways they are connected. Radiation explains why we talk of seemingly different things, such as wisdom and friendship, with the same metaphorical vehicles. Clustering explains why we use different metaphorical vehicles to deliver the same concept. Consider the target domain of *sports talk*. The following source domains, among others, are used commonly in English discourse because they cluster around the same target domain:

fortune

1. That team is very *lucky* to have won that game.

2. Their victory was *unpredictable; Fortune* must have been smiling on them.

war

3. They were soundly *defeated* in the first round of the play-offs.

4. That team has a good *attack* plan, but a poor *defense.*

chess

5. That goal came about because of that player's great *move.*

6. The use of that particular player as a *pawn* worked perfectly.

economics/value

7. That team *earned* a hard-fought tie.

8. That player's *worth* to the team is going up constantly.

eating

9. That team is *hungry* for a victory.

10. To win, you must have a *thirst* for victory.

thought system

11. Their *approach* to the game is excellent.

12. They now have a winning *mentality.*

The clustering of such source domains allows people to "hop" mentally from one source domain to the other, as they talk about sports: *The Milwaukee Brewers have a good game plan, but they often fail to implement it; they thus end up constantly in defeat; although one can claim that they have been very unlucky.* This statement makes sense only to those who are familiar with the above source domains. Such "domain hopping" is a prevalent feature of discourse, as the work in CMT has amply documented. It would seem that active participation in meaningful cultural discourses entails the ability to "hop around" source domains appropriately in response to specific communicative situations.

The function of radiation is a connective one. For example, the same source domain of the *journey* is used in English discourse to deliver such abstractions as *life, love,* and *friendship,* among others. This is why these topics are sensed to have a connectivity that others do not:

Life	Love	Friendship
My life is finally on the **right path**.	Their love is finally on the **right path**.	Their friendship is finally on the **right path.**
Your life has a **long way** to go.	Your love has a **long way** to go.	Your friendship has a **long way** to go.
Their life has **reached** a critical juncture.	Their love has **reached** a critical juncture.	Their friendship has **reached** a critical juncture.

There is a third type of metaphorological process that shapes group-think. It can be called *ordering*, and defined as the tendency to form different "orders" of conceptual metaphors, from lower-order ones, such as *seeing is believing (I have a different point of view, I never see eye to eye with him*, etc.), to higher-order ones such as the *think up* construction *(Where did you think that idea up?)* The lower the order of the conceptual metaphor, the more universal it tends to be; the higher its order the more culture-specific it is apt to be. The reason for this is that lower-order conceptual metaphors are built from source domains consisting mainly of sensory vehicles to implicate abstractions such as mentation *(thought, knowledge, discernment, understanding*, etc.). In evolutionary terms, the crystallization of such basic conceptual metaphors in human thought suggests that people across the world conceptualize thoughts within their minds in the same was that they perceive external objects with their sensory apparatus. As Walter Ong (1977, 134) has aptly remarked, this probably suggests that "we would be incapacitated for dealing with knowledge and intellection without massive visualist conceptualization, that is, without conceiving of intelligence through models applying initially to vision."

Lower-order conceptual metaphors are central to understanding the *raison d'être* of many rituals, traditions, values, and beliefs. For example, the *love is a sweet taste* conceptual metaphor *(She's my sweetheart, I love my honey*, etc.) is reified in love and romance rituals that reflect it in nonverbal ways: sweets are given to a loved one on St. Valentine's day; matrimonial love is symbolized at a wedding ceremony by the eating of a cake; lovers sweeten their breath with candy before kissing; and so on. Emantian (1995) has documented the same type of reification in various cultures. In Chagga, a Bantu language of Tanzania, the man is portrayed as the *eater* and the woman as his *sweet food*, as can be detected in expressions that mean, in translated form, "Does she taste sweet?" "She tastes sweet as sugar honey" (Emantian 1995, 168). In that culture, sweets also play a meaningful role in courtship and matrimonial practices.

Lower-order metaphors are also found commonly in mythic and religious narratives throughout the world. A common expression such as *He has fallen from grace* would have been recognized instantly in a previous era as referring to the Adam and Eve story in the Bible. Because we live in a secular society, today we continue to use it with only a dim awareness (if any) of its Biblical origins. Expressions that portray *life* as a *journey—I'm still a long way from my goal, There is no end in sight*, etc.—are similarly rooted in Biblical narrative. As the late Canadian literary critic Northrop Frye (1981) aptly pointed out, one cannot penetrate such expressions, or indeed most of Western literature or art, without having been exposed, directly or indirectly, to the original Biblical stories. These furnish the source domains for many of the conceptual metaphors we use today for judging human actions and offering advice, bestowing upon everyday life a kind of implicit metaphysical meaning and value.

Higher-order concepts are produced by the clustering of lower-order ones. As we saw in chapter 2, expressions such as *think up, think over, think out, think straight,* and *think through* result from the linkage of lower-level conceptual metaphors such as *ideas are viewable objects* with *ideas are objects that can be scanned.* Higher-order concepts such as these tend to be culture-specific, because they are built from pre-existing metaphorical linkages. This is why they are almost impossible to translate.

It should be mentioned, at this point, that not all groupthink is shaped by metaphorical processes. Some aspects of groupthink are influenced by the classificatory practices of a culture. The use of the alphabet is a case-in-point. Among other things, the alphabet allows us to organize books on shelves in libraries, or refer to them in bibliographies, according to the first letter of the name of the author or title. Books can be further organized according to subject area, according to the nature of the information, etc. The alphabetic mode of classification influences the way we do a host of other kinds of things, from creating indexes to organizing knowledge in devices as dictionaries and encyclopedias.

Some types of classification entail opposition—*A* vs. *B*, *yes* vs. *no*, etc. This process also shapes groupthink. If asked to define *good*, for example, we would tend to answer that it is the opposite of *evil*. We are inclined to do the same thing for a host of concepts—*night-day, sad-happy, hot-cold, good-bad,* etc. But opposition in itself does not tell the whole story, because it is often, itself, productive of metaphorical meaning, as the following chart shows:

Evil	*Good*	*Appropriate?*
an evil tyrant	a good tyrant	?
the evil effects of a poor diet	the good effects of a poor diet	no
evil omens	good omens	yes
an evil temper	a good temper	yes
evil news	good news	yes
an evil exterior paint	a good exterior paint	?
an evil joke	a good joke	yes
an evil drink	a good drink	?
evil taste	good taste	?
an evil table	a good table	?

Those expressions above that cannot be put into a simple binary opposition betray a metaphorical meaning: e.g., *a good table* means "a bountiful table," whereas *an evil table* implies that "evil people are at the table." Without going into a detailed discussion of the theory of opposition in psychology, suffice it to say that, as the above chart shows, oppositional relations never tell the whole story of how we process meaning because of the dominant role played by metaphor in the constitution of concepts.

Conceptual Productivity

A central problem of CMT research is determining which conceptual metaphors are more or less "productive" in a culture, i.e., are used to a greater or lesser degree for representational, ritualistic, and communicative purposes and activities. Is the concept of *love* more or less productive than, say, *justice* in our culture? That is to say, does the concept of *love* surface more often in texts, in discourses, and in social rituals than does the concept of *justice*? Is there a way of determining, or even "measuring," the relative productivity of these two concepts?

To the best of my knowledge, the question of conceptual productivity (henceforward CP) has never been identified as such, let alone examined, in the relevant CMT literature. The metric to be presented here is based on data related to two abstract concepts in English and Italian —*love* and *ideas* (Danesi, forthcoming). With a group of research assistants at the University of Toronto, a pilot project was initiated in early 2000 to fashion a technique for measuring the CP of these two concepts. The team gathered data from a variety of English and Italian written and oral texts (newspapers, magazines, popular books, radio, and television programs). From the data, a list of source domains was compiled. It was found, for example, that in English *ideas* was rendered consistently by such source domains as *moving things, light and darkness, buildings, plants, commodities, vision, geometry, food, people, fashion,* among others (as we have seen in this book).

On the basis of 100 texts, the research team found a cumulative number of 89 distinct source domains used to deliver the concept of *ideas* (or *thinking*) in English. This can be called its *Productivity Index* (PI = 89). Given the number of texts used, with regular statistical inference techniques it can be considered to be a reliable metric for this specific concept: i.e., there is no reason to believe that a compilation of similar data would yield significantly different results (within regular margins of statistical error). Some source domains were enlisted more frequently than others. This could, of course, be a matter of style (some types of texts tend to manifest the utilization of certain source domains more than others), or a true index of productivity within the target domain. The pilot project did not control for this aspect of CP. It emerged as a consequence of the study and, thus, is an issue that will have to be investigated in future work on CP. For the present purposes, the PI can be defined, simply, as an approximate indication of the productivity of a concept, given a specific sample of data.

The PI of *thinking* was then compared to the PI of *love* (using the same database). The latter manifested itself through the medium of such source domains as physics *(There were sparks between the two actors)*, health and disease *(The roles focused on the sick relationship between them)*, insane symptoms *(He's gone mad over her)*, magic *(She has bewitched her lover)*, among others. The PI for *love* was found to be 36. This suggests that *love* is, probably, a less productive concept than *thinking* in English. To compare the two, the notion of *Relative Productivity Index* (RPI) was introduced. This is defined, simply, as the quotient that emerges when the lower PI is divided into the higher one. In the data collected, this turns out to be 2.47 (RPI = 2.47). This means, in effect, that there are 2.47 more source domains used for delivering *thinking* than there are for delivering *love* in English, according to the data compiled.

What does this imply? It suggests, probably, that in English culture, *thinking* is a concept that is given much more representational salience than is *love*. This does not mean that the latter is not important, but, simply that there are fewer ways to conceptualize it in everyday cultural groupthink. It is left for future work to investigate whether differential RPIs lead to differences in cultural emphases.

The notion of CP can also be used to compare conceptual systems cross-culturally in a specific way. Knowledge of some of the source domains above—*food, people,* and *clothing*—is relatively independent of culture. However, there are some source domains that are dependent upon cultural knowledge. A comparative analysis will not only identify these, but also allow us to compare the RPI of certain concepts cross-culturally.

In the Italian data, it was found that most of the source domains used to deliver the concept of *thinking* were isomorphic. For example, as in English, geometrical figures *(Le loro idee sono parallele* "Their ideas are parallel")*, vision *(Non siamo stati capaci di vedere quello che voleva dire* "We weren't able to see what he wanted to say")*, food *(Le idee radicali di quel partito lasciano un sapore amaro in bocca* "The radical ideas of that party have left a bitter taste in our mouths")*, people *(Quel metodo scientifico è ancora nella sua infanzia* "That scientific method is still in its infancy")*, fashion *(Quell'idea è andata fuori moda anni fa* "That idea went out of fashion years ago")*, and others were frequent in the Italian data. However, the team found differences in semantic focus within a domain. For example, rather than *plants* (e.g., *That idea has many ramifications*), which also exists in Italian, the notion of *fertility* emerged as more productive in delivering the target domain of *ideas (Quella politica è arida* "That type of politics is arid"), as did *meteorological events (Le sue sono idee tempestose* "His ideas are tempestuous," *Piovono nuove idee in quell'università* "New ideas are raining in that university") and *weight (Una delle sue idee è, comunque, un'idea assai leggera* "One of his ideas is, however, quite light"). Overall, the Italian PI came to 123. The RPI between Italian and English in this domain was, therefore, 1.38 (which means that the Italian data showed 1.38 more source domains than the English data in the delivery of *ideas*). Needless to say, this is just an initial figure and would have to be tested again with other kinds of data. But, inferentially-speaking, there is no reason to believe that similar results would not emerge. The PI for *love* in Italian came to 99; and the RPI between *ideas* and *love* came to 1.24. Comparing the PIs for *love* in English and Italian, the RPI came to 2.75. This implies that there were almost three times as many source domains used to verbalize and represent *love* in the Italian data than there were in the English data.

When one talks about *ideas* or *love,* it is tantamount to "source-domain hopping," as we saw above, by which one passes (mentally) from *food* to *plants* to *buildings,* etc. producing stretches of discourse such as: *I cannot quite swallow that new theory, even though it is claimed to have many ramifications, and can lead to a new framework of understanding.* The notion of CP is, therefore, a predictor of what domains are more likely to be involved in the "hopping" process, and which concepts are likely to be more or less productive during it.

Related to the notion of PI is *Source Domain Productivity* (SDP). This provides a comparative measure of the vehicles utilized within source domains: e.g., the *seeing* source domain above is highly productive in English and Italian for the delivery of *ideas*; however, the *scanning* one is rather limited in both languages, since very few vehicles in the domain were selected to deliver the concept. The SDP of the former is thus higher than that of the latter in both languages: in English it is 25 and 5, in Italian 29 and 12 for *seeing* and *scanning* respectively. Once again, this suggests that some metaphorical vehicles are more frequent than are others. Within each source domain, there are subdomains that provide the concept-user with an array of specific vehicles that can be utilized to provide subtle detail to some concept. The higher the SDP, the more likely the utilization of that source domain.

The whole notion of CP can be extended to concepts that are forged metonymically and ironically, of course. In the English data, the PI for conceptual metonyms came to 12 for *ideas* and 4 for *love*; in the Italian data it came to 14 for *ideas* and 7 for *love*. This suggests that metonymy is much less a factor in discourse than is metaphor, although this finding too would have to be investigated further. In the English data, the PI for conceptual eireins came to 8 for *ideas* and 14 for *love*; in the Italian data it came to 9 for *ideas* and 10 for *love*. This suggests, again, that irony plays much less of a role in common discourse than does metaphor.

Concepts can also be compared in terms of source domains. If two concepts use identical source domains (in part or in whole), then they would have an identical PI. For example, *friendship* and *love* tend to be delivered in terms of identical (or similar) source domains, as part of their radiative structure (above):

depth

13. Theirs is a *profound* friendship/Theirs is a *profound* love.

duration

14. Theirs was a *brief* friendship/Theirs was a *brief* love affair.

directionality

15. Their friendship is *continuing on*/Their love affair is *continuing on*.

taste

16. Theirs is a *sweet* friendship/Their love is *sweet*.

The notion of CP has many applications and leads to the formulation of a set of interesting questions: Do concepts with a high PI have more reifications in cultural practices and customs than do those with a lower one? Does a source domain with a high SDP become a common one in discourse and in rituals? With the notion of CP, these and similar questions can now be formulated and researched empirically.

Metaform Theory

The term *metaform* was proposed by Sebeok and Danesi (2000) as a term to stand for any cultural form (a symbol, a representation, a ritual, a tradition, etc.) that is derived from a conceptual metaphor. A metaform is, in other words, an expressive or representational reification of either a specific conceptual metaphor, or of a subset of source domains that cluster around an ICM. Consider, as a case-in-point, the metaforms derived from several of the many source domains that cluster around the ICM of *love*:

physics

17. There were *sparks* between us.

18. We are *attracted* to each other.

19. My life *revolves* around her.

20. I am *magnetically drawn* toward her.

health and disease

21. Theirs is a *sick* relationship.
22. Their marriage is *dead*; it can't be *revived*.
23. Their relationship is in *good shape*.

insanity

24. I'm *crazy* about her.
25. He's constantly *raving* about her.
26. She's *gone mad* over him.
27. I've *lost my head* over her.

magic

28. She *cast a spell* over me.
29. The *magic* in our love is still there after so many years.
30. She has *bewitched* me.
31. I'm in a *trance* over her.

These conceptual metaphors are the source of the following practices and beliefs: (1) the use of fortune tellers and horoscopes to predict personal romance *(love is magic)*; (2) the medieval practice of bleeding people to "cure them" of their love *(love is a disease)*; (3) the belief that people who are in love lose their sense of reason and behave erratically *(love is insanity)*; and (4) the custom of lovers holding hands or embracing *(love is a physical attraction)*. These are beliefs and traditions that have literally "given form" to the above source domains. They are perfect examples of metaforms.

To grasp how metaforms materialize in groupthink, consider the use of the *rose* as a symbol for *love* in Western culture. The *rose* is a vehicle that occurs in three source domains that we use commonly to deliver the concept of *love*, namely *love is a sweet smell*, *love is a red color*, and *love is a plant*. It is, concretely speaking, a red plant with a sweet smell (Harvey and Shalom 1997). The *rose* symbol can now be seen to constitute a metaform derived from the clustering of three source domains designed to deliver the concept of *love*. It is a vehicle common to each of the three source domains.

Metaforms are so common that we hardly ever recognize their metaphorical origins. Take, as an example, metaforms derived from conceptual metaphors based on the *vision* source domain. These underlie, for example, the art of *chiaroscuro*—the technique of using light and shade in painting, invented by the Italian baroque painter Michelangelo Merisi da Caravaggio (1573–1610). They are also the source for the fact that "illumination" is emphasized by religions, and the reason why so-called "visionary" or "revelatory" experiences are regularly portrayed in terms of dazzling sensations of light. Metaforms derived from the *justice is blind* conceptual metaphor, to use another example, crop up commonly in pictorial representations, such as the statues of blindfolded women inside and outside courtrooms to stand for *justice*. And the *people are animals* conceptual metaphor is the source of such metaforms as the use of animals in totemic or heraldic traditions, in the creation of fictional characters children's narratives, in the naming of sports teams, and in the creation of surnames, to mention but a few:

Metaforms Derived from *People Are Animals*

Fictional Characters	Sports Teams	Surnames
Bugs Bunny	Chicago Bears	John Fox
Easter Bunny	Detroit Lions	Mary Cardinal
Snoopy	St. Louis Cardinals	Jane Wolf
Woodstock	Toronto Blue Jays	Mark Sparrow
etc.	etc.	etc.

Metaforms can also have a metonymic derivation. As an example, consider the *face is the person* conceptual metonym (chapter 3). Throughout the world, this concept is the reason why masks are used in many types of rituals. These are metaforms of personality. In ancient Greece, the word *persona* signified a "mask" worn by an actor on stage. Subsequently, it came to have the meaning of "the personality of the stage character," after masks were no longer used. This meaning can still be seen in the theater term *dramatis personae* "cast of characters" (literally "the persons of the drama"). Eventually, the word came to have its present meaning of "living human being." This explains why we continue to use "theatrical" expressions such as *to play a role in life, to put on a proper face*, etc. in reference to persons.

The mask metaform is an ancient one. Since at least Paleolithic times, people have used masks to cover the face, the entire head, or the head and shoulders for magical effect, because they are thought to represent deities, mythological beings, good and evil spirits, spirits of ancestors, animal spirits, and other entities presumed to possess power over humanity. In many tribal cultures, the shaman wears a mask during religious, healing, or curative rites, and is believed to be transformed into the spirit inhabiting or represented by the mask. Masks of human ancestors are often objects of family pride, and may be honored with ceremonies and gifts. In early agricultural societies, masks were worn to entice the heavens to send the rains. In hunting societies, animal masks were worn in rituals to ensure a successful hunt. Some societies think that masks are potentially dangerous unless handled with the proper rites. The Iroquois, for instance, carve their masks from a living tree, which must be ritually asked to grant permission for the carving and then must be offered tobacco.

The art of portraiture is another metaform of the *face is the person* metonym. It is the reason why the great portrait artists have always focused on the face as the bearer of personality. Portraits are probes of the face, designed to assay the many meanings that the "human mask" is capable of conveying. The first portraits of identifiable individuals date from Egypt around 3100 BC. These were mainly funereal representations of pharaohs and nobles. The subjects were seated in rigid, staring poses, communicating eternal authority. The ancient Romans made portraits of emperors that were remarkable in capturing the individuality of their subjects. Early Christian art, dating from the third to the seventh century, included portraits in mosaic and sculpted form. Known as *imago clipeatae,* the images of the subjects were generally stylized, relying on a standardized depiction of the face and the figure to convey authority. Medieval gospel books included portraits of the gospel authors, shown writing at their desks. During the same era, the portraits of donors became a means of verifying patronage, power, and virtue. The Renaissance marked a turning point in the history of portraiture. In that era artists started to become fascinated by the faces of average individuals. Rather than seeing portraiture as an art for depicting exceptional people, the artists saw it as a metaform for exploring the meaning of human character.

In sum, metaform theory suggests that metaphor is evidence of the human ability to visualize the universe as a coherent organism. Proof of our capacity, not just to see one thing in another but to change the very nature of things. When a metaphor is accepted as fact, it enters groupthink, taking on an existence in the real world.

Folk Wisdom

As reifications of conceptual metaphors, metaforms can also be seen to inform the repertory of sayings, proverbs, and other such verbal traditions that make up the *folk wisdom* of a culture. This is the generic term used in anthropology to indicate the insights on life and human behavior transmitted in a culture through its proverbs, aphorisms, humorous forms, and folktales. Although some of these may pass in and out of written literature and may cross over into oral tradition, an essential trait is their broad diffusion and their passage from one generation to another, largely by word of mouth. Throughout cultures, they are perceived intuitively as being timeless and revealing universal truths.

Part of folk wisdom is the strategic deployment of humor as a commentary on life. All cultures have their jokes and funny expressions that are meant to shed light on certain aspects of reality or human personality. These are, typically, metaforms of concepts that are either metaphorical, metonymic, or ironic in origin. Certain words are funny in the way they sound, like *bobble* and *squirt*, revealing the role of sound symbolism in the production of humorous metaforms (chapter 3). Puns also make us laugh because they play metaphorically or ironically on words, whereby one word is said when another one is meant.

Aphorisms, truisms, sayings, and proverbs are particularly relevant to the present discussion because they reveal how metaforms are used to provide sound practical advice when it is reckoned to be necessary in certain situations:

32. You've got too many fires burning (= advice to not do so many things at once).
33. Rome wasn't built in a day (= advice to have patience).
34. Don't count your chickens before they're hatched (= advice to be cautious).
35. An eye for an eye and a tooth for a tooth (= equal treatment is required in love and war).
36. Misery loves company (= depressed people are more likely to seek emotional support than are those who are not).

Every culture has similar proverbs. They constitute a remarkable code of ethics and of practical knowledge. Indeed, the very concept of *wisdom* implies the ability to apply proverbial language insightfully to a situation (Hoffman and Honeck 1987, Honeck 1997). Preaching, too, would hardly be persuasive were it not implanted on metaformal thinking. An effective preacher is one who knows how to structure his or her oration around a few highly understandable metaforms: e.g., *sex is dirty, sex is punishable by fire,* etc. These guide the preacher's selection of words, illustrations, turns of phrase, practical examples, etc.—*You must cleanse your soul of the filth of sex; You will burn in Hell, if you do not clean up your act.*

It is interesting to note that one of the most popular publications of the eighteenth century in America was an almanac, called *Poor Richard's Almanac,* written and published by Benjamin Franklin (1706–1790). Apparently, it became popular because it contained alluring proverbs that have since become household sayings in America. Franklin came to the idea of the almanac early in his career, when he was a printer and publisher in Philadelphia. He issued the almanac for every year from 1733 to 1758, writing under the name of Richard Saunders, an imaginary astronomer. Like other almanacs of its time, *Poor Richard* included such features as a horoscope, practical advice, jokes, poems, and weather predictions.

At first, *Richard* had little wit or humor. But as his character developed, he became a clever spokesman for Franklin's ideas on thrift, duty, hard work, and simplicity. *Poor Richard's Almanac* grew into one of the most popular and influential works printed in colonial America. Many of its sayings have become famous:

37. A penny saved is a penny earned.
38. God helps them that help themselves
39. Early to bed and early to rise makes a man healthy, wealthy, and wise

The almanac greatly influenced American thought before and after the Revolutionary War of 1775–1783. Franklin enlarged the almanac for the 1748 edition and called it *Poor Richard Improved*. In the preface to the final edition, published in 1757, he collected many of *Richard's* proverbs on how to succeed in business and public affairs. The preface, called "The Way to Wealth," was reprinted separately and was widely read in England and France, as well as in America.

The constant use of a proverb, a saying, or an aphorism leads to what is known as a *cliché*—an expression that has become trite through over-usage. Expressions such as *handwriting on the wall, many are called, few are chosen*, and *an eye for an eye* are all proverbs that have become clichés. From Shakespeare we get the following clichés: *a pound of flesh, method to my madness*, and *witching hour*. Despite their apparent triteness, we continue to use them because we still sense that they provide wisdom. They enable common people to quote the Bible or Shakespeare, whether they mean to or not, and thus to give implicit authority to their statements.

Discourse

Discourse is verbal interaction of various kinds. In all its manifestations, it constitutes an intricate social ritual that involves not only the deployment of implicit linguistic cues that are designed to keep a conversation going, but also an array of nonverbal signals that determine whose turn it is to speak and what goals are relevant in the enactment of the ritual. For discourse to be truly meaningful, however, it must be based on appropriate metaphorical reasoning, for this is the primary form of unconscious reasoning that connects the discourse situation to cultural groupthink.

Consider the following anecdotal scenario in which a typical high school student is saying good-bye, first to his English teacher, second to his mother, and third to a peer (Danesi 2003):

Good-bye to English Teacher: Good-bye, sir!

Good-bye to Mother:	See ya' later, ma!
Good-bye to a Peer:	I gotta' split, man!

The student's statements are not interchangeable—i.e., the adolescent would not say *I gotta split, man!* to a teacher, and vice versa, he would not say, *Good-bye, sir!* to a peer. This simple, yet instructive, example shows that the choice of language forms and the types of discourse patterns that are utilized in specific situations will vary along a social dimension. This kind of knowledge is known in the standard literature as *pragmatic* or *discourse competence*. Now, a closer metaphorological analysis of the three variants of "good-bye" reveals that the speaker employed a specific type of metaform in each situation to convey different types of social meanings. The *See ya' later, ma* expression reifies the expectation that the speaker, being an adolescent, is anticipated back home by the mother. The *I gotta' split, man* expression reifies the fact that teenagers form close affective bonds, which they must, from time to time, "split."

The above example reveals how metaphorical meanings are built into discourse, even if, as in the case above, the expressions are highly ritualized and thus, probably unconscious. Lack of knowledge of the appropriate metaform would entail a "meaning asymmetry" whereby only a "set formula" is used or a wrong one applied to the situation at hand. This is, in fact, what happens when the speaker is someone who has learned a language as a foreign learner. Discourse is not a simple matter of a formulaic information exchange, nor is it generated in an arbitrary fashion. Rather, it is highly interconnected with the metaformal structure of cultural groupthink, thus ensuring that the ways in which people talk to each other in their social spheres are regular and fluid.

Metaforms also regulate the zones people maintain between each other and the ways they orient their bodies when interacting in discourse situations (Hall 1966). For example, when strangers are introduced to each other in our culture, each one knows not only to extend the right hand to initiate a handshake, but also how far to stand from the other person. They would also not tend to touch any other part of the other person's body—arms, face, etc.—other than the right hand during the handshake. The source for such metaforms is the perception of *space* as an extension of *Selfhood*. This is why we call any breach of a culturally-appropriate distance during greeting rituals a *breach of personal space*. This metaform is also reified in common expressions such as the following:

40. Keep your *distance*.
41. They're very *close*.
42. We've drifted *far apart*.
43. You're trespassing into my *personal space*.

44. I can't quite *get to him*.

45. Please keep in *touch*.

The anthropologist Desmond Morris (1969) claims that handshaking may have originated as a way to show that neither person was holding a weapon. It thus became a "tie sign," because of the bond it was designed to establish. Throughout the centuries, this sign evolved into a symbol of equality among individuals, being used to seal agreements of all kinds—a meaning it has retained to this day. Indeed, refusing to shake someone's outstretched hand would be interpreted as a sign of aggressiveness or as a challenge. Predictably, this greeting metaform reveals a high degree of cross-cultural variation. People can squeeze the hand (as Europeans and North Americans do), shake the other's hand with both hands, shake the hand and then pat the other's back or hug him or her, lean forward or stand straight while shaking, and so on.

Anthropologists are unclear as to why such metaforms vary so much across cultures. In my opinion, it is due to differing perceptions of the Self—which come out in metaphorical expressions related to Selfhood. People in some cultures seem to think of themselves as literally "contained" in their skin. The zones of privacy that define "Self-space" in such cultures, therefore, include the clothes that cover the skin. In other cultures, the Self is felt to be located down within the body shell. As a consequence, people in these cultures are in general more tolerant of crowds, of noise levels, of the touching of hands, of eye contact, and of body odors than most North Americans are (Hall 1966).

In a truly interesting book on the use of discourse in clinical therapeutic situations, Linda Rogers (1998) provides strong evidence that the function of discourse is, in effect, to "express the Self." In therapy sessions with one particular troubled and disabled patient, JR, Rogers used the *journey* metaform to great advantage to help him learn how to do this in a socially-acceptable fashion. JR came to her because he had sought work over a three-year period that was consistent with his real abilities, but could never get the job he wanted. Rogers discovered that his lack of success was not due to any lack of skill, but rather, to the fact that he could not negotiate social discourse successfully. The *journey* metaform —in which his life was compared by Rogers to a journey—allowed JR to understand what the underlying problem was through metaphorical reasoning. Rogers was thus able to help JR out of his dilemma by bringing him to the realization that, in expressing himself in discourse, he had to abide by specific rules of cultural groupthink. Rogers' approach turned out to be a truly effective strategy, in my view, because discourse is steeped in what the sociologist Erving Goffman (1959) called the "presentation of the Self" in socially-acceptable ways. Using a series of techniques (video interviews, informal meetings), Rogers was able to make JR aware of this very fact. As a consequence, JR developed the ability to consciously modulate and adjust his speech in a strategic fashion.

In another case, Rogers used a similar technique to help a patient named Sarah overcome a deep trauma that resulted from being shot at by a deeply disturbed man while she was waiting for her husband to pick her up outside a university building. Rogers was in the building at the time teaching a class and, therefore, was able to run to her rescue, saving Sarah by applying artificial respiration and by talking to her. As her patient, Rogers helped Sarah recover from her emotional wounds by getting her to narrate the incident over and over—an incident from which she wanted to dissociate herself completely, as if it never happened. In her narratives Sarah, a special educator, saw herself as wanting to help her assailant, who was later shot dead by the police during a confrontation. Sarah's internal discourse with her assailant revolved around how she would have helped him understand himself, and thus come to grips with his emotional confusion. But in her internal dialogue, the assailant was always a silent partner. Thus, her narrative was hardly cathartic. As a result, Sarah sought another kind of solution—changing her Self by changing her body. Sarah chose tattooing as a way to redesign her persona. Using the same metaform of the *journey* that Rogers used with JR, she was able to help Sarah come to the view that she could only come to grips with the situation by changing her *path* and starting a new *journey*. As in the case of JR, the strategy worked.

Such anecdotal case studies make it rather obvious that communication is a complex phenomenon that involves an interconnection between the Self, the situation, and culture. As the foregoing discussion makes evident, for discourse to be appropriate it must reify metaforms that connect the speech situation to the broader frame of cultural meanings implicit in it. Metaforms, moreover, unconsciously structure the flow of a conversation. The following brief stretch of recorded conversation between two students on the University of Toronto campus shows how the *people are animals* concept did this (Sebeok and Danesi 2000, 128–129):

Student 1: You know, that prof is a real *snake*.

Student 2: Yeah, I know, he's a real *slippery* guy.

Student 1: He somehow always knows how to *slide* around a tough situation.

Student 2: Yeah, tell me about it! Keep away from his courses; he bites!

The associative chain of thought that this metaform triggered in that conversation can be represented as follows:

snake → *slippery* → *slide* → *bites*

Sometimes, the conversational flow is shaped not by a single source domain, but by a series of domains, which are interconnected through clustering. In one conversation about *ideas*, an interlocutor made use of the following sequence of source domains (Sebeok and Danesi 2000, 129): *ideas are seeing → ideas are food → ideas are fashion → ideas are persons*:

> I do not *see* how anyone can *swallow* his ideas, especially since most of them have gone *out of fashion*, and thus are *dying*.

The Poetic Origin of Culture

Anthropologists trace the origin of culture to the fashioning of tools, a feat that was accomplished at least 2.5 million years ago, and to the use of gesture for communication. Gradually, planned hunting, fire-making, the weaving of cloth, and the ritualized burial of the dead became well-established characteristics of human cultures. By about 100,000 years ago, the making of art, vocal communication, and communally-established systems of ethics emerged to make thinking and planning consciously and transmitting skills and systems of social relationships to subsequent generations through language systematic and efficient in a cultural setting.

Although interest in culture is as old as human history, the first scientific definition of culture had to await the nineteenth century, when the British anthropologist Edward B. Tylor (1832–1917) characterized culture as a communal system of beliefs that are expressed and represented in specific ways (through language, rituals, etc.) (Tylor 1871). Tylor also made a crucial distinction between *culture* and *society*. Although these terms continue to be used commonly as synonyms in many languages, in actual fact they refer to different things. Within a social collectivity, there can, and frequently does, exist more than one culture. In an opposite manner, several societies can be thought of as belonging to the same general culture—e.g., European culture, Asian culture, African culture, etc. The Polish-born British anthropologist Bronislaw Malinowski (1884–1942) argued that cultures came about so that humans could solve similar basic physical and moral problems the world over (Malinowski 1922, 1923, 1929). He claimed that the symbols, languages, rituals, and institutions that humans created, no matter how strange they might at first seem, had universal signifying properties built into them that allowed people everywhere to solve similar life problems. The brilliant Swiss psychologist Carl Jung (1875–1961) saw cultures as springing from a *collective unconscious* of primordial images that gained physical form in the systems of expression and representation that are found in cultures across the world (Jung 1921, 1956, 1957, 1965). He called the images *archetypes*. Take, for example, the "trickster" archetype. In every person there exists a predilection for puerile mischief. So, at the personal level, the trickster archetype may manifest itself as a desire for frivolity, as playing devil's advocate in a discussion, as a sly craving to mock someone's success, as an urge to steal something for the sheer thrill of it, and so on. At a cultural level, it may manifest itself in myths, legends, poetry, paintings, stories, and the like. In Western culture, for instance, the trickster surfaces as Dickens's *Artful Dodger*, as the fabled character known as *Rumpelstiltsken*, as Shakespeare's Puck in *A Midsummer Night's Dream*, in the character assumed by many modern-day comedians, and so on and so forth.

Vico saw culture as a product of poetic logic. He pointed out that word *culture* is itself an agrarian metaphor (from Latin *cultus*, past participle of *colere* "to till"). Culture is, in effect, a memory system that preserves what the poetic imagination has invented. It transforms *sensory knowing* into *communal knowing*. Evidence of this transformation can, of course, be found in metaphor and, more specifically, in the metaforms of a culture. This is why everything in a culture has metaphorical meanings. Take, as an example, buildings. Beyond shelter, buildings are constructed to encode social meanings. Temples, churches, and mosques, for instance, are designed to allow people to celebrate the mysteries of religion and to provide assembly places where spiritual meanings can be given expressive form. Palaces, villas, and skyscrapers are designed to display power and wealth. Architectural practices, in effect, reify concepts of social organization and lifestyle in specific metaphorical ways. Consider, for example, the height of a building. The cities built during the medieval period had one outstanding architectural feature—the tallest building noticeable along their skyline was the church's spire, which rose majestically up towards the sky. This design feature symbolized the power and wealth of the clergy. In our secular culture today, however, the tallest buildings in sprawling urban centers are not churches. In cities like Dallas, Toronto, Montreal, New York, Chicago, and Los Angeles the tallest buildings are owned by large corporations and banks. Wealth and power now reside literally and symbolically in these institutions. Inside these mammoth structures the social dynamics also mirror an *up-down* image schema: the jobs and positions with the lowest value are at the bottom of the building; the more important ones are at the top. The company's executives reside, like the gods on Mount Olympus, on the top floor. This architectural symbolism is the reason why we use such metaphorical expressions as *to work one's way up, to make it to the top, to climb the ladder of success, to set one's goals high,* etc.

Cities too are imbued with metaphorical meanings. Their design reflects cultural values, beliefs, and emphases. In ancient Greece, for instance, religious and civic citadels were oriented in such a way as to give a sense of aesthetic balance to the inhabitants—streets were arranged in a grid pattern and housing was integrated with commercial and defense structures. In Renaissance Europe, city planners stressed wide, regular radial streets forming concentric circles around a middle point, with other streets radiating out from that point like spokes of a wheel. To this day, the downtown core is known as *centro* in Italy, reflecting this Renaissance practice of building cities in the shape of circles.

After the Industrial Revolution the concept of the grid started to gain a foothold on city designs. The grid system conveys efficiency of movement and facility of localization. But since the middle part of the twentieth century, many new city designs have emerged. Hotels and other recreational buildings (e.g., casinos) are taking on some of the power symbolism that has been associated with the banks and the corporations. The city of Las Vegas is a classic example of a city designed to cater to the craving for recreation and consumption. The tall hotel towers that mark its landscape are symbols of a world of fast money, quick recreational fixes, and consumerist delights.

In sum, as examples such as this suggest, the components of culture are imbued with metaphorical meanings because culture itself is, as Vico claimed, the cumulative product of metaphorical thinking as guided by poetic logic. Culture is thus both restrictive and liberating. It is restrictive in that it imposes upon individuals born into a specific culture an already-fixed system of metaforms. This will largely determine how people come to understand the world around them. But culture is also liberating because, paradoxically, it provides the means by which individuals can seek new meanings on their own. This is why ideas are constantly being modified by new generations of artists, scientists, philosophers, and all kinds of folk, producing new ways in which everyone can think of and experience reality.

Chapter 5

INTERCONNECTEDNESS

Words convey the mental treasures
of one period to the generations
that follow; and laden with this,
their precious freight, they sail
safely across gulfs of time in which
empires have suffered shipwreck
and the languages of common life
have sunk into oblivion.
— Anonymous

The study of metaphor is ultimately a study in how thought, language, and culture are intertwined in a seamless "poetic" amalgam of meaning-making—an amalgam that we come to use from childhood onwards to understand reality and our place within it. The main objective of this book has been to argue, primarily by illustration, that metaphor is a trace to the nature of that amalgam. This is, in my view, the most important lesson to be learned from Vico's *New Science*. The most consequential implication of this lesson is that human ideas and institutions mirror the poetic "modifications" of the human mind, as Vico put it:

> For the first indubitable principle posited above is that this world of nations has certainly been made by men, and its guise must therefore be found within the modifications of our own human mind. And history cannot be more certain than when he who creates the things also narrates them (Bergin and Fisch 1984, 349).

In this final chapter, I will discuss the notion of the interconnectedness of thought, language, and culture, since it brings out, perhaps better than anything else, what the notion of poetic logic is all about.

The Interconnectedness Principle

In the previous chapter, metaform theory was introduced as a framework for studying the material and behavioral reifications of conceptual metaphors. That framework allowed us to investigate how language, symbolism, artistic practices, social rituals, and all the other forms of meaning-making that constitute a culture are connected to each other. Metaform theory is, clearly, based on an implicit *interconnectedness principle*, which posits that cultural expressions, symbols, representations, and traditions are interconnected to each other through metaphorical reasoning. To quote Baudrillard one more time (preface), such reasoning allows us to make the world "visible" and, thus, understandable in concrete ways.

Take, as an example, the interconnectedness between language, myth, magic, and religion. From the beginning of time, language has been thought to have special magical powers. This perception is woven into the prayers, formulas, incantations, and litanies of all religions, which are seen as capable (potentially at least) of curing disease, warding off evil, bringing good to oneself, and so on. In many early cultures, even knowing the name of a deity was purported to give the knower great power—e.g., in Egyptian mythology, the sorceress Isis tricked the sun god, Ra, into revealing his name and, thus, allowing her to gain power over him and all other gods. In some cultures, the name given to the newborn child is thought to bring with it all the qualities of the previous individuals who shared that name, weaving a sort of magical protective aura on the individual named after them. The Inuit, for instance, believe that a newborn baby cries because it wants its ancestral name, and will not be complete until it gets it. In some tribes, an individual will refuse to utter his or her name, fearing that this senseless act of "breath-wasting" could break the magical spell of protection that the name brings with it. As Espes Brown (1992, 13) puts it: "the fact is that when we create words we use our breath, and for these people and these traditions breath is associated with the principle of life; breath is life itself. And so if a word is born from this sacred principle of breath, this lends an added sacred dimension to the spoken word."

Belief in the magical powers of language is not limited to tribal cultures. It exists even in modern secular societies, albeit in a latent unconscious fashion. *Speak of the devil,* we say in common parlance, and *he will appear,* without being consciously aware of what we are saying. When someone sneezes, we utter *Bless you,* probably unaware of its meaning as an imploration to divine providence to ward off sickness. As Ann Gill (1994, 106) aptly puts it, language is still felt to be magical because even in secular societies words create things:

By portraying experience in a particular way, words work their unconscious magic on humans, making them see, for example, products as necessary for success or creating distinctions between better or worse– be it body shape, hair style, or brand of blue jeans. Words create belief in religions, governments, and art forms; they create allegiances to football teams, politicians, movie stars, and certain brands of beer. Words are the windows of our own souls and to the world beyond our fingertips. Their essential persuasive efficacy works its magic on every person in every society.

As another example, consider how a single image schema, [verticality], is capable of shaping various practices, rituals, etc. in our own culture. In verbal discourse, for example, it manifests itself in expressions such as: *I'm feeling up; They're feeling down; I'm working my way up the ladder of success; His status has gone down considerably;* etc. As a metaform, it surfaces in religious narratives, where heaven is located in the skies and hell below the earth. In public building design, too, it can be discerned in the fact that the taller office buildings in a modern city are the ones that indicate which institutions (and individuals) hold social and economic power. In musical composition, higher tones are typically employed to convey a sensation of happiness, lower ones of sadness. During speech, the raising of a hand designates notions of amelioration, betterment, growth, etc., whereas the lowering of the hand designates the opposite notions. In bodily representation and perception, this metaform shows up in the common viewpoint that *taller is more attractive/shorter is less attractive.* In mathematical and scientific representational practices its instantiation can be seen, for instance, in the ways in which graphs are laid out—lines that are oriented in an upward direction indicate a growth or an increase of some kind, while those that are slanted in a downward direction indicate a decline or decrease. The list of instantiations of the [verticality] schema could go on and on. It is the imaginary element that interconnects different domains of symbolism and representation, imparting a commonality of sense to them.

As a final example, consider sports events. These have great emotional meaning in modern-day secular cultures because they are interconnected with a fundamental mythological theme—good (the home team) vs. evil (the visiting team). This is why the whole fanfare associated with preparing for the "big event," such as the Superbowl of American football, has a ritualistic quality to it similar to the ritualistic pomp and circumstance that ancient armies engaged in before going out to battle and war. The symbolism of the home team's (army) uniform, the valor and strength of the players (the heroic warriors), and the skill and tactics of the coach (the army general) all have a powerful effect on the fans (the two warring nations). The game (the battle) is perceived to unfold in moral terms, as a struggle between the forces of good and evil. Sports figures are exalted as heroes or condemned as villains. This train of thought, incidentally, comes out constantly in sports talk. Following are statements that I recorded from American TV broadcasts that show this:

1. The *Forty-Niners* lost the final battle.
2. The *Giants'* quarterback has fallen from his lofty perch, hasn't he?
3. The *Yankees* are always looked upon favorably by the sports gods.
4. That period of hockey was a titanic struggle for the home side.

The interconnectedness of sports to myth is, in effect, what gives meaning to sport spectacles, and to many other spectacles for that matter. When people move to a different culture, they have a difficult time coming to grips with the new spectacles, not because they are radically different in purpose from those to which they were accustomed in the culture in which they were reared, but because they do not see the interconnectedness of meanings that they embody. They are thus experienced as isolated events and, thus, ascribed little or no emotional value.

Symbolism

As argued in the previous chapter, metaformal reasoning underlies the production of certain kinds of symbolism. The conceptual metonym the *face is the person* (chapter 3) is a perfect case-in-point. From the beginning of time, human beings have perceived the face to be a conveyor of Selfhood. This is why ritualistic alterations to the face at puberty are found throughout the world and across time, given that puberty is the point in the lifecycle where the child is expected to construct an appropriate social persona. For example, the pubescent males of the Secoya people who live along the Río Santa Naría in Peru wear a sprig of grass through their nasal septum (the partition that divides the two nasal cavities) for the traditional circumcision rite of passage. When a young man becomes a father for the first time in some tribal Gê societies of Brazil, he must insert a saucer-like plate, which may reach a diameter of four inches, through the flesh of his lower lip to symbolize his passing from boyhood to manhood. Although Westerners might consider such forms of facial alteration mutilating, one must not forget Western practices like ear-piercing, nose-piercing, and even straightening, capping, or bleaching the teeth—all of which might appear just as mutilating to other peoples.

Another perfect case-in-point of interconnectedness is food symbolism. Expressions such as *bread of life* and *earning your bread* abound in many languages, revealing the metaphorical linkage of *bread* with *life*. This is why many of the symbolic meanings of food are interconnected with mythic and religious accounts of human origins. The Christian story of Adam and Eve, for instance, revolves around the eating of an apple. In actual fact, the Hebrew account of the Genesis story tells of a forbidden fruit of knowledge, not an apple. The representation of this fruit as an apple can be traced to medieval Christian visual depictions of the Eden scene, when painters and sculptors became interested in the Genesis story. The symbolism of the apple as a "knowledge fruit" continues to resonate in our culture. This is why the apple tree symbolizes the "tree of knowledge;" why the Apple Computer company has chosen this fruit as its logo; and so on.

Predictably, food symbolism produces effects on our perception of the foods themselves. The fact that in our culture rabbits, cats, and dogs, for instance, are perceived to be household pets, impels us to perceive cooked rabbit, cat, and dog meat as inedible. On the other hand, we eat bovine (beef steaks, hamburgers, etc.), lamb, and poultry meat routinely, with no discomfort. Such cultural perceptions are not universal. In India, a cow is classified as sacred and, therefore, as inedible. Incidentally, this is the basis of our expression *sacred cow* to refer to something unassailable and revered. Anglo-American culture does not classify foxes or dogs as edible food items, but the former is reckoned a delicacy in Russia, and the latter a delicacy in China.

Edibility is, clearly, more a product of Culture than it is of Nature. Outside of those that have a demonstrably harmful effect on the human organism, the types of flora and fauna that are considered to be edible or inedible vary greatly among different cultures. Perceptions of edibility have largely a basis in history, not digestive processes. If we were left alone on an island, the criterion we would use for edibility would certainly not be one based on taste, but of survival at any taste. We cannot get nourishment from eating tree bark, grass, or straw. But we certainly could get it from eating frogs, ants, earthworms, silkworms, lizards, and snails. Most people in our society would, however, respond with disgust and revulsion at the thought of eating those things. This notwithstanding, there are societies where they are not only eaten for nourishment, but also considered to be delicacies.

In sum, we perceive gustatory differences in cuisine as fundamental differences in worldview and lifestyle. Our expression *to develop a taste* for some food reveals how closely tied edibility is to interconnected cultural meaning-making. One must always keep in mind that there simply are no universal canons of "good taste." In our society we eat fish with great enjoyment, but we do not eat the eyes of fish, which we find distasteful, by and large. But those living in many other societies do. To see others eat the eyes tends to cause discomfort or queasiness within some of us. It is a small step from this unpleasant sensation to a misguided perception of the eaters as "tasteless."

Description

One of the everyday functions of metaphor, as has been implicit in many of the illustrations used in this book, is that of "gap filling." In a fundamental sense, metaphor is a "verbal drawing technique" that allows people to describe referents for which there are no adequate words available. In all cases, both the content and the style of the metaphorical description is interconnected with culture-specific systems. Take, for example, the domain of Euclidean geometry. In Western culture the various ideas and concepts of this type of geometry have become habits of mind, because of the simple fact that it has been taught to children in school since the beginning of obligatory education. No wonder, then, that geometrical terms are being constantly used as descriptors for a whole range of referents that allow people to characterize them in some fashion. For example, in baseball, a ball hit with a certain amount of force, but without gaining much height, is described as a *line* drive; baseball players are said to *circle* the bases after hitting a home run; and so on. Such descriptors are really higher-order metaphors (chapter 4) that can only be used or understood by people who have knowledge of Euclidean geometry. The use of second-order metaphors derived from school subjects is, in actual fact, a salient feature of common discourse. Here are a few examples of this:

from mathematics

5. *Add* this on to the list of things to do.
6. You should *divide* your work load *up* more equally.
7. He has a *calculating* mind.
8. That whole thing is worth *zero*.

from the sciences

9. There is good *chemistry* among the players on that team.
10. Those ideas *crystallized* at the right time.
11. Try to *filter out* all those negative thoughts from your mind.
12. That theory *evaporated* into thin air.

from reading

13. To understand what she means you must *read between the lines*.

14. You must always *cross* your T's and *dot* your I's.
15. Please *spell out* what you mean.
16. You must always read the *fine print* in all things.

There are many descriptive strategies of this kind that we use so regularly that they have become habits of thought, having lost their image schematic import. All this shows that when we do not have the appropriate lexical structures and formulas available to describe something, we invariably resort to culture-specific source domains to fill-in the gaps. One of the sources to which we now tend to turn is that of media terminology. The following examples show how conditioned we have become to the use of such terminology:

from print media
17. He has a great *character*.
18. I cannot *read* your mind.
19. Make a mental *note* of what I just said.
20. It is time too turn over a new *leaf*.
21. His life is an open *book*.
22. You must start over *tabula rasa*.
23. Her story is *written* in my heart.

from electronic, photographic, and filmic media
24. I just had a *flashback*.
25. What mental *picture* do these words evoke?
26. My mind is out of *focus*.
27. He has a *photographic memory*.
28. I am going over what you said in *slow motion*.

from the computer medium
29. He is *hard-wired* for action.
30. My mental *software* no longer works.
31. I can't quite *retrieve* that memory.
32. I haven't yet *processed* what he said.
33. Did your *store* away what I told you?

Such expressions overlap constantly in discourse, leading to various kinds of reifications. For instance, the use of computer terminology today to describe everything from the human mind to so social activities has had many reifications in pop culture and in the literary and cinematic arts. Movies about robotic beings have even taken on a "family-friendly" orientation, as can be seen in some of the movies produced by the Disney Corporation. On the other hand, the domain of computers has necessitated metaphorical gap-filling in its own right, with, for instance, terms from the navigational source domain—*navigating the web, surfing the web,* etc. All this shows, in effect, is that cultures are interconnected systems of meanings. As digital technologies continue to advance, so too will the use of their attendant terminologies to describe human activities. The interconnectedness of technology to the pulse of everyday life is something that comes out constantly in the language of our times.

Gesture

Another case-in-point that illustrates the interconnectedness principle is gesture. Gesture is symbolic and communicative behavior involving the hands, the arms, and to a lesser extent, the head. It is characteristic of humans and primates. Chimpanzees raise their arms in the air as a signal that they want to be groomed; they stretch out their arms to beg or invite; and they have the ability to point to things in similar ways to humans (Beaken 1996, 51). These gestures are, evidently, purposeful and regulatory of the actions of other chimps. But the number of gestural forms of which chimpanzees are capable is limited. Human gesturing, on the other hand, is productive, varied, and highly interconnected to other meaning-making systems (Bremer and Roodenburg 1991; Armstrong, Stokoe, and Wilcox 1995; Emmorey and Reilly 1995). This comes out concretely in the manual forms that people produce spontaneously across cultures to accompany speech. As the research of the linguist David McNeill (1992) has shown, such forms are intrinsically interconnected with the contents of messages. After videotaping a large sample of people as they spoke, McNeill found that the gestures that accompany speech, which he called *gesticulants,* reify the conceptual system inherent in oral discourse. This suggested to him that speech and gesture constitute a single integrated referential/communication system that allows a person to get the message across effectively.

McNeill classified the gesticulants into five main categories. First, there are *iconic* gesticulants, which, as their name suggests, bear a close resemblance to the referent or referential domain of an utterance: e.g., when describing a scene from a story in which a character bends a tree back to the ground, a speaker observed by McNeill appeared to grip something and pull it back. His gesture was, in effect, a visual metaform of the action talked about, revealing both his memory image and his point of view (he could have taken the part of the tree instead).

Second, there are *metaphoric* gesticulants. These are also visual, but their content is abstract, rather than purely iconic. For example, McNeill observed a male speaker announcing that what he had just seen was a cartoon, simultaneously raising up his hands as if offering his listener a kind of object. He was obviously not referring to the cartoon itself, but to the genre of the cartoon. His gesture represented the genre as if it were an object, placing it into an act of offering to the listener. This type of gesticulant typically accompanies utterances that contain expressions such as *presenting an idea, putting forth an idea, offering advice*, and so on.

Third, there are *beat* gesticulants. These resemble the beating of musical tempo. The speaker's hand moves along with the rhythmic pulsation of speech, in the form of a simple flick of the hand or fingers up and down, or back and forth. Beats are metaforms marking the introduction of new characters, summarizing the action, introducing new themes, etc. during the utterance.

Fourth, there are *cohesive* gesticulants. These serve to show how separate parts of an utterance are supposed to hold together. Beats emphasize sequentiality, cohesives globality. Cohesives can take iconic, metaphoric, or beat form. They unfold through a repetition of the same gesticulant form, movement, or location in the gesture space. It is the repetition itself that is meant to convey cohesiveness.

Fifth, there are *deictic* gesticulants. Deixis is the term used by linguists to designate pointing or indicating signs. Deictic gesticulants are aimed not at an existing physical place, but at an abstract concept that had occurred earlier in the conversation. These reveal that we perceive concepts as having a physical location in space. For example, when uttering *You cannot do that*, the tendency is to point to *that* with the index finger in the gesture space as if it were a place within it.

McNeill's work gives us a good idea of how the gestural mode of representation is interconnected with the vocal one in discourse. As Frutiger (1989, 112) has also observed, accompanying gestures reveal an inner need to support what one is saying orally: "If on a beach, for example, we can hardly resist drawing with the finger on the smooth surface of the sand as a means of clarifying what we are talking about."

Basically, gesture allows speakers to reify concepts in physical ways: e.g., the deployment of circular hand movements when talking of a circle reifies the *ideas are geometrical figures* concept; the moving of both the head and hands in an upward direction when talking about such things as *rising prices* reifies the *up is better* concept; and so on and so forth. The image schematic source of gestural forms is also evident in *sign languages*. The spatial and orientational use of hand movements, as well as facial expressions and body movement, constitute the "delivery mode" of sign languages. In American Sign Language (ASL), for instance, the sign for "catch" involves one hand (in the role of agent) moving across the body (an action) to grasp the forefinger of the other hand (the patient). ASL gestural forms are made by one or both hands, which assume distinctive shapes and movements.

Sign languages are also used by hearing peoples for various purposes. One of the best-known examples is the sign language developed by the Plains peoples of North America as a means of communication between tribes with different languages. For example, the manual sign for a white person is made by drawing the fingers across the forehead, indicating a hat. Special manual signs are used for particular rivers, mountains, and other natural features. The sensation of cold is indicated by a shivering motion of the hands in front of the body; and the same sign is used for winter and for year, because the Plains peoples count years in terms of winters. Slowly turning the hand, relaxed at the wrist, means vacillation, doubt, or possibility; a modification of this sign, with quicker movement, is the question sign. This sign language is so elaborate that a detailed conversation is possible using the gestures alone (Mallery 1972).

Science and Mathematics

Scientific and mathematical concepts, too, reveal an interconnected structure. Science is an attempt to render visible with our poetic minds those things we can never see with our eye—atoms, sound waves, gravitational forces, magnetic fields, etc. The trace to this "inner vision" is, of course, metaphor. This is why sound waves are said to *undulate* through empty space like water waves ripple through a still pond; atoms to *leap* from one quantum state to another; electrons to *travel in circles* around an atomic nucleus; and so on. The physicist K. C. Cole (1984, 156) puts it as follows:

> The words we use are metaphors; they are models fashioned from familiar ingredients and nurtured with the help of fertile imaginations. "When a physicist says an electron is like a particle," writes physics professor Douglas Giancoli, "he is making a metaphorical comparison like the poet who says 'love is like a rose.'" In both images a concrete object, a rose or a particle, is used to illuminate an abstract idea, love, or electron.

As Robert Jones (1982, 4) has also pointed out, for the scientist metaphor serves as "an evocation of the inner connection among things." It is interesting and relevant to note that the philosopher of science, Fernand Hallyn (1990), has identified the goal of science as that of giving the world a "poetic structure."

As a concrete example of how the scientist uses poetic logic to construct ideas, consider the origin of atomic theory again. As discussed briefly in the opening chapter, it was Ernest Rutherford who first speculated that atomic structure mirrors the solar system—a theory that reified, in effect, the ancient Greek concept of the cosmos as having the same structure at all its levels, from the microcosmic (the atom) to the macrocosmic (the universe). It is mind-boggling to think that such a simple conceptual linkage has led to real knowledge about matter. It appears that the poetic brain is a discovery organ—an organ designed to seek hidden pattern through connections based on sense implication.

This can be seen especially in the discoveries brought about serendipitously by mathematical thinking (Lakoff and Nuñez 2000; Lave 1988; Reed 1994; English 1997). As a case-in-point, take a famous mathematical puzzle formulated by Leonardo Fibonacci (c. 1170–c. 1240) in his *Liber Abaci*, published in 1202. Fibonacci designed his book as a practical introduction to the Hindu-Arabic numeral system, which he had learned to use during his extensive travels in the Middle East. He wanted to show Europeans, who were accustomed to using the cumbersome Roman numeral system, how simple it was to solve simple problems with the Hindu-Arabic system. The puzzle in question is found in the third section of the *Liber Abaci:*

> A certain man put a pair of rabbits, male and female, in a very large cage. How many pairs of rabbits can be produced in that cage in a year if every month each pair produces a new male-female pair which, from the second month of its existence on, also is productive?

The solution goes somewhat as follows. There is 1 pair of rabbits in the cage at the start. At the end of the first month, there is still only 1 pair, for the puzzle states that a pair is productive only "from the second month of its existence on." It is during the second month that the original pair will produce its first offspring pair. Thus, at the end of the second month, a total of 2 pairs, the original one and its first offspring pair, are in the cage. Now, during the third month, only the original pair generates another new pair. The first offspring pair must wait a month before it becomes productive. So, at the end of the third month, there are 3 pairs in total in the cage—the initial pair, and the two offspring pairs that the original pair has thus far produced. If we keep tabs on the situation month by month, we can show the sequence of pairs that the cage successively contains as follows: 1, 1, 2, 3. The first digit represents the number of pairs in the cage at the start; the second, the number after one month; the third, the number after two months; and the fourth, the number after three months.

During the fourth month, the original pair produces yet another pair; so too does the first offspring pair. The other pair has not started producing yet. Therefore, during that month, a total of 2 newborn pairs of rabbits are added to the cage. Altogether, at the end of the month there are the previous 3 pairs plus the 2 newborn ones, making a total of 5 pairs in the cage. This number can now be added to our sequence: 1, 1, 2, 3, 5. During the fifth month, the original pair produces another newborn pair; the first offspring pair produces a pair as well; and now the second offspring pair produces its own first pair. The other rabbit pairs in the cage have not started producing offspring yet. So, at the end of the fifth month, 3 newborn pairs have been added to the 5 pairs that were previously in the cage, making the total number of pairs in it: 5 + 3 = 8. We can now add this number to our sequence: 1, 1, 2, 3, 5, 8. Continuing to reason in this way, it can be shown that after twelve months, there are 233 pairs in the cage. Now, the intriguing thing about this puzzle is the sequence of pairs itself:

$$1, 1, 2, 3, 5, 8, 13, 21, 34, 55, 89, 144, 233$$

The salient characteristic of this sequence is that each number in it is the sum of the previous two: e.g., 2 (the third number) = 1 + 1 (the sum of the previous two); 3 (the fourth number) = 1 + 2 (the sum of the previous two); etc. Known as the *Fibonacci sequence*, it can of course be extended ad infinitum, by applying the simple rule of continually adding the two previous numbers to generate the next:

$$1, 1, 2, 3, 5, 8, 13, 21, 34, 55, 89, 144, 233, 377, 610, 987, ...$$

Little did Fibonacci know how significant his sequence would become. There is, in fact, no evidence to suggest that he knew about his own sequence. Its remarkable properties were discovered first (to the best of my knowledge) by the French mathematician François Edouard Anatole Lucas (1842–1891) over six centuries later. For the present purposes, suffice it to say that it has been found to conceal many unexpected mathematical patterns, For example, if the nth number in the sequence is x, then every nth number after x turns out to be a multiple of x:

- the third number is 2, and every third number after 2 (8, 34, 144, ...) is a multiple of 2;
- the fourth number is 3, and every fourth number after 3 (21, 144, 987, ...) is a multiple of 3;
- the fifth number is 5, and every fifth number after 5 (55, 610, ...) is a multiple of 5.

More significantly, the sequence surfaces unexpectedly in Nature and in human activities: e.g., daisies tend to have 21, 34, 55, or 89 petals (= the eighth, ninth, tenth, and eleventh numbers in the sequence); trilliums, wild roses, bloodroots, columbines, lilies, and irises also tend to have petals in Fibonacci sequence; a major chord in Western music is made up of the octave, third, and fifth tones of the scale, i.e., of tones 3, 5, and 8 (another short stretch of consecutive numbers in the Fibonacci sequence). The list of such reifications is truly astounding.

Why would the solution to a simple puzzle reveal patterns in the real world? There is, to the best of my knowledge, no definitive answer to this question; nor can there ever be one. As mathematician Ian Stewart puts it (2001, v), for some mysterious reason "simple puzzles could open up the hidden depths of the universe." The astounding "predictive power" of mathematics lies, arguably, in the fact that the type of poetic thinking used to create puzzles reifies hidden connections among real things. Perhaps, as puzzles suggest, the human brain is designed to discover patterns in the world serendipitously because it already has such patterns built into it (Danesi 2002).

A classic example of how poetic thinking guides mathematical discovery is Euclid's proof that the prime numbers are infinite. The integers are divided into those that can be decomposed into factors—*composite numbers*—and those that cannot. The numbers 12, 42, and 169, for instance, are all composite because they are the products of smaller numbers, called factors: e.g., $12 = 2 \times 2 \times 3$, $42 = 7 \times 2 \times 3$, $169 = 13 \times 13$. The *prime numbers* are those that cannot be decomposed in this way. They are the factors in composite numbers. The first ten primes are: {2, 3, 5, 7, 9, 11, 13, 17, 19, 23}. Now, even a cursory examination of the number line—{0, 1, 2, 3, 4, 5, 6, 7, 8, 9, 10, ...}—reveals that there are fewer and fewer primes on it as the numbers increase. Thus, it appears *logical* to conclude that the primes must come to an end at some point. "Common sense" would also have it that if a number is big enough, it must be the product of smaller prime factors. But, with a blend of poetic and deductive thinking, Euclid proved that this is not so.

He started with the assumption that there may indeed be a finite set of primes, labeling them as follows: $\{p_1, p_2, p_3, \ldots p_n\}$. The symbol p_n stands for the last (largest) prime. Concretely, the set would look like this: $\{2, 3, 5, 7, 9, \ldots p_n\}$. Euclid then had one of the illuminations that comes from poetic thinking: What kind of number would result from multiplying all the primes in the set: $\{p_1 \times p_2 \times p_3 \times \ldots \times p_n\}$? The result would, of course, be a composite number because it can be factored into smaller prime factors—p_1, p_2, etc. Then, with a flash of insight, Euclid added 1 to this product: $(p_1 \times p_2 \times p_3 \times \ldots \times p_n) + 1$. Call this number N $(= p_1 \times p_2 \times p_3 \times \ldots \times p_n + 1)$. Clearly, N is not decomposable, because when any of the prime factors available to us $\{p_1, p_2, p_3, \ldots p_n\}$ are divided into it, a remainder of 1 would always be left over. So, the number N is either: (1) a prime number that is obviously much greater than p_n, or (2) a composite number with a prime factor that, as just argued, cannot be found in the set $\{p_1, p_2, p_3, \ldots p_n\}$ and is thus also greater than p_n. Either way, there must always be a prime number greater than p_n. In this way, Euclid showed that the primes never end.

Euclid's proof puts on display the power and mysterious appeal of poetic thinking. Incidentally, ever since its publication, Euclid's proof has motivated myriads of mathematicians to come up with a formula for generating the prime numbers—but so far to no avail. Prime numbers are the "building blocks" of the whole architecture of arithmetic. In a letter to the great mathematician Leonhard Euler in 1742, the mathematician Christian Goldbach (1690–1764) conjectured that every even integer greater than 2 could be written as a sum of two primes (Salem, Testard, and Salem 1992, 110–111):

$$4 = 2 + 2 \qquad 8 = 5 + 3 \qquad 12 = 7 + 5 \qquad 16 = 11 + 5$$
$$6 = 3 + 3 \qquad 10 = 7 + 3 \qquad 14 = 11 + 3 \qquad 18 = 11 + 7$$

etc.

No exception is known to *Goldbach's Conjecture*, as it has come to be known, but we have no valid proof of it. Goldbach also conjectured that any number greater than 5 could be written as the sum of three primes:

$$6 = 2 + 2 + 2 \quad 8 = 2 + 3 + 3 \quad 10 = 2 + 3 + 5$$
$$7 = 2 + 2 + 3 \quad 9 = 3 + 3 + 3 \quad 11 = 3 + 3 + 5$$

etc.

In his delightful novel, *Uncle Petros and Goldbach's Conjecture* (2000), the Greek writer Apostolous Doxiadis treats *Goldbach's Conjecture* as one of those "revelations" provided occasionally by God to mystify human ingenuity, even if it is doubtful that, should a proof of the conjecture ever be revealed, it would change the world in any way.

But some proofs and discoveries have indeed changed the world. One of these was the constant π—the ratio of the circumference of a circle to its diameter. This ratio is the same for every circle and is approximately 3.14159. The digits in π go on forever and no patterns seem to characterize the infinite sequence. Today, π has been calculated to over 8 billion digits! The fascinating thing is that, in the process of calculating π, mathematicians have come across many other kinds of patterns that have led to significant discoveries in number theory, trigonometry, and computer programming techniques. The mysterious qualities of this number were even explored cinematically by Darren Aronofsky in his brilliant film π: *Faith in Chaos* (1997), which deals with mathematician Maximilian Cohen's search for an elusive numerical code hidden in π, as he teeters on the brink of insanity. Cohen is on the verge of the most important discovery of his life—decoding the numerical pattern beneath the seemingly random and chaotic stock market figures—when he is accosted by a Wall Street firm set on financial domination and a Kaballah sect intent on unlocking the secrets behind their ancient holy texts. Cohen races to crack the code, discovering the presence of π in it as a key to unlocking the secret of existence.

The question that the movie raises is a profound one. Did Maximilian, through a flash of insight, stumble serendipitously upon some truly mysterious hidden pattern in π that provides a key to understanding the mystery of life? The movie does not, of course, provide an answer, adding to the sense of mystery it enfolds. The word *serendipity*, incidentally, was coined by Horace Walpole in 1754, from the title of the Persian fairy tale "The Three Princes of Serendip," whose heroes make many fortunate discoveries accidentally. Serendipity characterizes the history of mathematics and is, arguably, the reason why we believe mathematics can bring about change in that world. The Pythagoreans, as is well known, believed that mathematics mirrored the inherent order in the universe. Incidentally, so petrified of chaos were they that they considered their "theory of order" seriously undermined when, ironically, Pythagoras's own theorem revealed the existence of irrational numbers such as $\sqrt{2}$. This "chaotic" number stared them straight in the face each time they drew an isosceles right-angled triangle with equal sides of unit length. The length of its hypotenuse was the square root of the sum of $1^2 + 1^2$, or $\sqrt{2}$, a number that cannot be represented as the ratio of two integers, or as a finite or repeating decimal (it begins 1.4142136...). For the Pythagoreans, rational numbers had a "rightness" about them; irrational ones such as $\sqrt{2}$ did not. And yet, there they were, defying logic and sense, and challenging the system of order that the Pythagoreans so strongly desired to establish. So disturbed were they that, as some stories have it, they suppressed their discovery of $\sqrt{2}$, going to the length of killing one of their own colleagues for having committed the sin of letting the nasty information reach the world.

Incredibly, even in the domain of chaos, poetic logic finds ways of making sense of things. *Chaos theory*, founded by French mathematician Henri Poincaré (1854–1912), has shown, in fact, that there are patterns even in random events. In the early 1960s, simplified computer models demonstrated that there was a hidden structure in the seemingly chaotic patterns of weather. When these were plotted in three dimensions they revealed a butterfly-shaped fractal set of points. Similarly, leaves, coastlines, mounds, and other seemingly random forms produced by Nature reveal hidden fractal patterns when examined closely.

All this constitutes a truly profound paradox. Why is there order in chaos? Perhaps the ancient myths provide, after all, the only plausible response to this question. According to the *Theogony* of the Greek poet Hesiod (eighth century BC), Chaos generated Earth, from which arose the starry, cloud-filled Heaven. In a later myth, Chaos was portrayed as the formless matter from which the Cosmos was created. In both versions, it is obvious that the ancients felt deeply that order arose out of chaos. For some truly mysterious reason, our mind requires that there be order within apparent disorder.

The foregoing discussion makes it clear why the early history of mathematics overlaps considerably with myth and mysticism. Numerology started with the Pythagoreans, who taught that all things were numbers, and that all relationships could be expressed numerically. In the ancient Hebrew world, too, it was believed that the letters of any word or name found in sacred scripture could be interpreted as digits and rearranged to form a number that contained secret messages encoded in it. The earliest recorded use of the art of *gematria*, as it was called, was by the Babylonian king Sargon II in the eighth century BC, who built the wall of the city of Khorsbad exactly 16,283 cubits long because this was the numerical value of his name.

A thick volume could be written about the many meanings interconnected with specific numbers across the world and across history. Consider the mystical meanings ascribed to the number 7. It is found, for instance, in the Old Testament where, as part of God's instructions to Moses for priests making a blood offering we find the following statement: "And the priest shall dip his finger in the blood, and sprinkle of the blood seven times before the Lord, before the veil of the sanctuary" (Leviticus 4:6). It is also noteworthy that God took six days to make the world and then rested on the seventh. The number 13, too, has a long history of interconnectedness with mysticism. So widespread is the "fear of the number 13" in our culture that it has even been assigned a name: *triskaidekaphobia*. In Christianity, 13 is linked with the Last Supper of Jesus and his twelve disciples and the fact that the thirteenth person, Judas, betrayed Jesus. Other similarly "unlucky numbers" exist in different parts of the world. And across cultures, people tend to think of certain things such as dates, street addresses, or certain numbers as having great significance. As Rucker (1987, 74) aptly phrases it, human beings seem to possess the "basic notion that the world is a magical pattern of small numbers arranged in simple patterns."

It was only after the Renaissance that numerology was relegated to the status of a pseudoscience. Paradoxically, the Renaissance at first encouraged interest in the ancient magical arts. Intellectuals such as Italian philosopher Giovanni Pico della Mirandola (1463–1494) rediscovered the occult roots of classical philosophy, and protoscientists such as Swiss physician Philippus Aureolus Paracelsus (1493–1541) affirmed these practices. Both the Roman Catholic Church and the new Protestantism, however, turned sharply against numerology in the fifteenth and sixteenth centuries. Mathematics was subsequently completely liberated from the occult mysticism in which it was shrouded in the ancient world.

But the interconnectedness between mysticism and mathematics has hardly been lost. Observing a mysterious manifestation of Fibonacci numbers in Nature continues to cast a "magical spell" over us. In fact, to this day, the boundaries between mathematics and magic are rarely clear-cut. Every mathematical idea is caught up in a system of references to other ideas, patterns, and designs that humans are inclined to dream up. And this imparts an aura of Pythagorean mysticism to that very system.

In sum, in science and mathematics poetic logic reigns supreme. Scientific theories and mathematical principles are "miniature blueprints" of how pattern is wired into the brain and of how we search for answers to existential questions through poetic reasoning. This is not to imply that discoveries in mathematics and science are not just curious figments of mind. Rather, they are elusive bits of evidence of a theory of the world that is lurking around somewhere, but that seems to evade articulation.

The Quest for Meaning

The main goal of this book has been to take the reader on an excursion through an amalgam of facts, ideas, and illustrations that reveal how poetic logic works in making the world visible and thus understandable in human terms. Metaphor is a trace to poetic thinking, which constantly creates connections among things. This is why metaphors and metaforms have such emotional power—they tie people together, allowing them to express a common sense of purpose in an interconnected fashion.

Aristotle's metaphor *Life is a stage*, which he devised for his pupil to make life understandable (chapter 1), has, in effect, much more philosophy about life packed in it than do entire treatises. It suggests, among other things, that there is a "script" to life, written by a "a divine author," thus soothing our inbuilt fear of extinction. The idea of a life script without an author is a modern one. It has been represented brilliantly by modern dramatists such as Luigi Pirandello (1867–1936), in his play *Six Characters in Search of an Author* (1921), where the fantasy characters of a play are in desperate search of an author to "write them into existence," and Samuel Beckett (1906–1989) in his play *Waiting for Godot* (1952). The latter is a powerful indictment of the perceived wretchedness of the human condition. It continues to have great appeal because, like the two tramps in the play, many people today seem to have become cynical about the meaning of human existence, searching, like Pirandello's characters, for some author behind the scenes. The play portrays life as an absurd moment of consciousness on its way to extinction. But despite the play's nihilism, people seem paradoxically to discover meaning in it. Deep inside us, as audience members, we yearningly hope that Beckett is wrong, and that on some other stage, in some other play, the design of things will become known to us.

Waiting for Godot questions traditional assumptions about certainty and truth. It satirizes language, portraying it as a collection of words that can refer only to other words to have any meaning at all. It also deconstructs classic theater, which drew its stories and characters from myth. The objective of the ancient dramas was to consider humanity's place in the world and the consequences of individual actions. The classical actors wore costumes of everyday dress and large masks. Movement and gesture were stately and formal. The plots emphasized supernatural elements, portraying how humans and the gods struggled, interacted, and ultimately derived meaning from each other. Similarly, medieval morality plays put on display principles of human conduct that informed the populace about what was meaningful to existence. Shakespeare's great tragedies continued on in this vein. *Waiting for Godot* is a critique of this kind of meaning-making theater. The ancient dramas portrayed a world full of metaphysical meanings. *Godot* portrays a world in there is only a void, and where human beings fulfill no particular purpose in being alive. Life is a meaningless collage of actions on a relentless course leading to death and to a return to nothingness. In reply to Aristotle's *Life is a stage* metaphor, Beckett's play asserts that *Life is a farce*. But Beckett's bleak portrait of the human condition somehow forces us to think about that very condition, paradoxically stimulating in us a profound reevaluation of the meaning of life.

As Vico claimed, our quest to have life be a meaningful search was the originating force of history, producing belief systems by which natural events in the world were thought to be under the dominion of awesome and frightful gods—hence the emergence of sacred institutions and practices (religion, burial rites, the family) that constituted the foundations of culture. This "age of the gods," as he called it, eventually gave way to a succeeding "age of heroes," in which people with great physical prowess became leaders, inspiring fear and awe in the common people. After a period of domination by the heroes, a third stage—the "age of equals"—invariably crystallizes in which the common people rise up and win equality; but in the process the culture begins to disintegrate. This is because the third age is one of subtle irony and wit. Language becomes shallow and does not reflect the passions; it is a language of logical concepts, method, and reasoning devoid of its poetic, metaphorical functions. The ironic intellect is a destructive one, leading to a demise of the culture and either to a reversion to one of its earlier stages or to its reinvention.

The Vichian theory of culture strongly suggests that the evolution of *Homo sapiens* has been shaped by forces that we will never understand.

Indeed, for no manifest genetic reason, humanity is constantly reinventing itself as it searches, across time and geography, for a purpose to its existence. It is unlikely that we will ever know what these forces are. As quantum physicists found out at the start of the twentieth century, since theories are formulated with language, it is unlikely that the truth about the universe will ever be known. In quantum theory, the verbal description simply does not seem to fit what the mathematical equations say is going on. The substrate of physical reality appears to obey a logic utterly foreign to verbal concepts. People think of a particle, like a photon or an electron, as occupying space at a certain point in time, and traveling along a specific path. As it turns out, however, a particle does not really exist until it interacts with something, and it travels down not one path but all possible paths at once. Language came about to help people to get around on the earth, not the mysterious world of subatomic physics. So, too, with all other theories of reality. No theory formulated in language can ever penetrate the world of reality. It can however, as discussed in this book, reveal it serendipitously, through metaphor.

The subtext of this book has been that the answer which Aristotle gave his pupil to the question *What is life?* (chapter 1) reveals how each one of us attempts to answer life's biggest questions—with metaphorical insight. Aristotle's metaphorical response, *Life is a stage*, is the only truly meaningful response he could have given. Metaphor is the default form of thought, providing many angles from which to literally "see" the world. This is why any and all alternative metaphorical answers to the question posed to Aristotle would make sense—*Life is a bowl of cherries, a struggle, an adventure, a puzzle, a test*, etc. In a real sense, these are reifications of miniature philosophies about life, providing vital clues to understanding how we think about life and how we act in the real world. Someone who perceives *life* as an *adventure* is likely going to approach events differently from someone who perceives it as a *struggle*. Metaphors are not right or wrong. However, as we have seen throughout this book, they have consequences for how people think and act—consequences that are implicit in the metaphors themselves. As Aristotle and Vico certainly knew, metaphor is our best clue for understanding human thought, language, and culture.

WORKS CITED

Allwood, J., and P. Gärdenfors, eds. 1998. *Cognitive semantics: Meaning and cognition.* Amsterdam: John Benjamins.

Alverson, H. 1991. Metaphor and experience: Looking over the notion of image schema. In *Beyond metaphor: The theory of tropes in anthropology*, edited by J. W. Fernandez. Palo Alto, CA: Stanford University Press. 94–117.

Andrews, E. 1990. *Markedness theory.* Durham, NC: Duke University Press.

Andrews, E., and Y. Tobin, eds. 1996. *Toward a calculus of meaning: Studies in markedness, distinctive features, and deixis.* Amsterdam: John Benjamins.

Apel, K. O. 1975. *L'idea di lingua nella tradizione dell'Umanesimo da Dante a Vico.* Bologna: Il Mulino.

Aristotle. 1952a. *Poetics.* Vol. 11 of *The works of Aristotle*, edited by W. D. Ross. Oxford: Clarendon Press.

———. 1952b. *Rhetoric.* Vol. 11 of *The works of Aristotle*, edited by W. D. Ross. Oxford: Clarendon Press.

Armstrong, D. F., W. C. Stokoe, and S. E. Wilcox. 1995. *Gesture and the nature of language.* Cambridge: Cambridge University Press.

Arnheim, R. 1969. *Visual thinking.* Berkeley and Los Angeles: University of California Press.

Asch, S. 1950. On the use of metaphor in the description of persons. In *On expressive language*, edited by H. Werner. Worcester, MA: Clark University Press. 86–94.

———. 1958. The metaphor: A psychological inquiry. In *Person perception and interpersonal behavior*, edited by R. Tagiuri and L. Petrullo. Palo Alto, CA: Stanford University Press. 28–42.

Austin, J. L. 1962. *How to do things with words.* Cambridge: Harvard University Press.

Barbe, K. 1995. *Irony in context.* Amsterdam: John Benjamins.

Barcelona, A., ed. 1999. *Metaphor and metonymy at the crossroads: A cognitive perspective.* Berlin: Mouton de Gruyter.

Barrett, W. 1986. *The death of the soul: From Descartes to the computer.* New York: Anchor.

Basso, K. H. 1990. *Western Apache language and culture: Essays in linguistic anthropology.* Tucson: University of Arizona Press.

Battistella, E. L. 1990. *Markedness: The evaluative superstructure of language.* Albany: State University of New York Press.

Battistini, A. 1995. *La sapienza retorica di Giambattista Vico.* Milan: Guerini.

Baudrillard, J. 1987. *The ecstasy of communication*. St. Louis, MO: Telos Press.

Beaken, M. 1996. *The making of language*. Edinburgh, England: Edinburgh University Press.

Bergin, T. G., and M. Fisch. [1948] 1984. *The new science of Giambattista Vico*. Ithaca, NY: Cornell University Press.

Berlin, I. 1976. *Vico and Herder: Two studies in the history of ideas*. New York: Viking.

Bickerton, D. 1969. Prolegomena to a linguistic theory of metaphor. *Foundations of Language* 5: 34–52.

Billow, R. M. 1975. A cognitive developmental study of metaphor comprehension. *Developmental Psychology* 11: 415–423.

Black, M. 1962. *Models and metaphors*. Ithaca, NY: Cornell University Press.

Bloomfield, L. 1933. *Language*. New York: Holt, Rinehart, and Winston.

Boas, F. 1940. *Race, language, and culture*. New York: Free Press.

Bonfante, G. 1980. Vico e la linguistica. *Bollettino del Centro di Studi Vichiani* 10: 134–138.

Bonner, J. T. 1980. *The evolution of culture in animals*. Princeton, NJ: Princeton University Press.

Boole, G. 1854. *An investigation of the laws of thought*. New York: Dover.

Booth, W. 1979. Metaphor as rhetoric: The problem of evaluation. In *On metaphor*, edited by S. Sacks. Chicago: University of Chicago Press. 47–70.

Bottini, G. et al. 1994. The role of the right hemisphere in the interpretation of figurative aspects of language: A positron emission tomography activation study. *Brain* 117: 1241–1253.

Brakel, A. 1983. *Phonological markedness and distinctive features*. Bloomington: Indiana University Press.

Bremer, J., and H. Roodenburg, eds. 1991. *A cultural history of gesture*. Ithaca, NY: Cornell University Press.

Bronowski, J. 1977. *A sense of the future*. Cambridge: MIT Press.

Brown, R. W. 1958a. How shall a thing be called? *Psychological Review* 65: 14–21.

———. 1958b. *Words and things*. New York: The Free Press.

———. 1970. *Psycholinguistics*. New York: The Free Press.

Brown, R. W., R. A. Leiter, and D. C. Hildum. 1957. Metaphors from music criticism. *Journal of Abnormal and Social Psychology* 54: 347–352.

Brownell, H. H. 1988. Appreciation of metaphoric and connotative word meaning by brain-damaged patients. In *Right hemisphere contributions to lexical semantics*, edited by C. Chiarello. New York: Springer. 19–32.

Brownell, H. H., H. H. Potter, and D. Michelow. 1984. Sensitivity to lexical denotation and connotation in brain-damaged patients: A double dissociation? *Brain and Language* 22: 253–265.

Bühler, K. [1908] 1951. On thought connection. In *Organization and pathology of thought*, edited by D. Rapaport. New York: Columbia University Press. 81–92.

Cameron, L., and G. Low. 1999. *Researching and applying metaphor*. Cambridge: Cambridge University Press.

Casad, E. H., ed. 1996. *Cognitive linguistics in the Redwoods: The expansion of a new paradigm in linguistics*. Berlin: Mouton de Gruyter.

Cherry, C. 1957. *On human communication*. Cambridge: MIT Press.

Cherwitz, R., and J. Hikins. 1986. *Communication and knowledge: An investigation in rhetorical epistemology*. Columbia: University of South Carolina Press.

Chomsky, N. 1957. *Syntactic dtructures*. The Hague: Mouton.

———. 1964. Degrees of grammaticalness. In *The structure of language*, edited by J. A. Fodor and J. J. Katz. Englewood Cliffs, NJ: Prentice-Hall. 384–389.

———. 1986. *Knowledge of language: Its nature, origin, and use*. New York: Praeger.

———. 2000. *New horizons in the study of language and mind*. Cambridge: Cambridge University Press.

———. 2002. *On nature and language*. Cambridge: Cambridge University Press.

Churchland, P. M. 1988. *Matter and consciousness*. Cambridge: MIT Press.

Cienki, A., B. J. Luka, and M. B. Smith. 2001. *Conceptual and discourse factors in linguistic structure*. Stanford, CA: CSLI Publications.

Cole, K. C. 1984. *Sympathetic vibrations*. New York: Bantam.

Connor, K., and N. Kogan. 1980. Topic-vehicle relations in metaphor: The issue of asymmetry. In *Cognition and figurative language*, edited by R. P. Honeck and R. R. Hoffman. Hillsdale, NJ: Lawrence Erlbaum Associates. 238–308.

Crawford, C. 1988. *The beginnings of Nietzsche's theory of language*. Berlin: Mouton de Gruyter.

Damasio, A. R. 1994. *Descartes' error: Emotion, reason, and the human brain*. New York: G. P. Putnam's Sons.

Danesi, M. 1989. Vico and Chomsky: On the nature of creativity in language. *New Vico Studies* 7: 28–42.

———. 1990. Thinking is seeing: Visual metaphors and the nature of abstract thought. *Semiotica* 80: 221–237.

———. 1993. *Vico, metaphor, and the origin of language*. Bloomington: Indiana University Press.

———. 1995. *Giambattista Vico and the cognitive science enterprise*. New York: Peter Lang.

———. 2001. Light permits knowing: Three metaphorological principles for the study of abstract concept-formation. *Semiotica* 136: 133–149.

———. 2002. *The puzzle instinct: The meaning of puzzles in human life*. Bloomington: Indiana University Press.

———. 2003. *My son is an alien: A cultural portrait of contemporary youth*. Lanham, MD: Rowman and Littlefield.

———. Forthcoming. Metaphors and conceptual productivity. *Semiotica*.

Danesi, M., and D. Santeramo. 1995. *Deictic verbal constructions*. Urbino, Italy: Centro Internazionale di Semiotica e di Linguistica.

Davis, P. J., and R. Hersh. 1986. *Descartes' dream: The world according to mathematics*. Boston: Houghton Mifflin.

Deane, P. 1992. *Grammar in mind and brain: Explorations in cognitive syntax*. Berlin: Mouton de Gruyter.

Descartes, R. 1637. *Essaies philosophiques*. Leiden, Netherlands: L'imprimerie de Ian Maire.

Di Cesare, D. 1988. Sul concetto di metafora in Giambattista Vico. In *Prospettive di storia della linguistica*, edited by L. Formigari and F. Lo Piparo. Rome: Edizioni Riuniti. 213–224.

———. 1993. Parola, lógos, dabar: linguaggio e verità della filosofia di Vico. *Bollettino del Centro di Studi Vichiani* 22–23: 251–287.

———. 1995. Verum, factum, and language. *New Vico Studies* 13: 1–13.

Di Pietro, R. J. 1976. *Language as human creation.* Washington, DC: Georgetown University Press.

Dirven, R., and M. Verspoor. 1998. *Cognitive exploration of language and linguistics.* Amsterdam: John Benjamins.

Doxiadis, A. 2000. *Uncle Petros and Goldbach's conjecture.* London: Faber and Faber.

Dundes, A. 1972. Seeing is believing. *Natural History* 81: 9–12.

Eco, U. 1976. *A theory of semiotics.* Bloomington: Indiana University Press.

———. 1984. *Semiotics and the philosophy of language.* Bloomington: Indiana University Press.

Edie, J. M. 1976. *Speaking and meaning: The phenomenology of language.* Bloomington: Indiana University Press.

Emantian, M. 1995. Metaphor and the expression of emotion: The value of cross-cultural perspectives. *Metaphor and Symbolic Activity* 10: 163–182.

Emmorey, K., and J. Reilly, eds. 1995. *Language, gesture, and space.* Hillsdale, NJ: Lawrence Erlbaum Associates.

English, L. D., ed. 1997. *Mathematical reasoning: Analogies, metaphors, and images.* Mahwah, NJ: Lawrence Erlbaum Associates.

Espes Brown, J. 1992. Becoming part of it. In *I become part of it: Sacred dimensions in native American life,* edited by D. M. Dooling and P. Jordan-Smith. New York: Harper Collins. 1–15.

Fauconnier, G. 1985. *Mental spaces.* Cambridge: Cambridge University Press.

———. 1997. *Mappings in thought and language.* Cambridge: Cambridge University Press.

Fauconnier, G., and M. Turner. 2002. *The way we think: Conceptual blending and the mind's hidden complexities.* New York: Basic.

Fauconnier, G., and E. Sweetser, eds. 1996. *Spaces, worlds, and grammar.* Chicago: University of Chicago Press.

Fillmore, C. J. 1997. *Lectures on deixis.* Stanford, CA: CSLI Publications.

Firth, J. R. 1957. *Papers in linguistics: 1934-1951.* Oxford: Oxford University Press.

Fogelin, R. J. 1988. *Figuratively speaking.* New Haven, CT: Yale University Press.

Frege, G. 1879. *Begiffsschrift eine der Arithmetischen nachgebildete Formelsprache des reinen Denkens.* Halle, Germany: Verlag Louis Nebert.

Frutiger, A. 1989. *Signs and symbols.* New York: Van Nostrand.

Frye, N. 1981. *The great code: The Bible and literature.* Toronto: Academic Press.

Gardner, H. 1982. *Art, mind, and brain: A cognitive approach to creativity.* New York: Basic.

———. 1985. *The mind's new science: A history of the cognitive revolution.* New York: Basic.

Gentner, D. 1982. Are scientific analogies metaphors? In *Metaphor: Problems and perspectives,* edited by D. S. Miall. Atlantic Highlands, NJ: Humanities Press. 106–132.

Gibbs, R. W. 1994. *The poetics of mind: Figurative thought, language, and understanding.* Cambridge: Cambridge University Press.

Gill, A. 1994. *Rhetoric and human understanding.* Prospect Heights, IL: Waveland Press.

Goffman, E. 1959. *The presentation of self in everyday life.* Garden City, NY: Doubleday.

Grice, H. P. 1975. Logic and conversation. In *Syntax and semantics,* Vol. 3, edited by P. Cole and J. Morgan. New York: Academic Press. 41–58.

Gumpel, L. 1984. *Metaphor reexamined: A non-Aristotelian perspective.* Bloomington: Indiana University Press.

Hall, E. T. 1966. *The hidden dimension.* New York: Doubleday.

Halliday, M. A. K. 1973. *Explorations in the functions of language.* London: Edward Arnold.

———. 1975. *Learning how to mean: Explorations in the development of language.* London: Edward Arnold.

———. 1985. *Introduction to functional grammar.* London: Edward Arnold.

Hallyn, F. 1990. *The poetic structure of the world: Copernicus and Kepler.* New York: Zone Books.

Harvey, K., and C. Shalom, eds. 1997. *Language and desire: Encoding sex, romance, and intimacy.* London: Routledge.

Haskell, R. E. 1989. Analogical transforms: A cognitive theory of the origin and development of equivalence transformations. *Metaphor and Symbolic Activity* 4: 247–277.

Hausman, C. R. 1989. *Metaphor and art.* Cambridge: Cambridge University Press.

Herder, J. G. 1784. *Outlines of a philosophy of the history of mankind.* Translated by T. Churchill. London: Johnson.

Hier, D. B., and J. Kaplan. 1980. Verbal comprehension deficits after right hemisphere damage. *Applied Psycholinguistics* 1: 270–294.

Hinton, L., J. Nichols, and J. J.Ohala, eds. 1994. *Sound symbolism.* Cambridge: Cambridge University Press.

Hobbes, T. [1656] 1839. *Elements of philosophy.* London: Molesworth.

Hoffman, R. R. 1980. Metaphor in science. In *Cognition and figurative language,* edited by R. P. Honeck and R. R. Hoffman. Hillsdale, NJ: Lawrence Erlbaum Associates. 25–46.

Hoffman, R. R., and R. P. Honeck. 1980. A peacock looks at its legs: Cognitive science and figurative language. In *Cognition and figurative language,* edited by R. P. Honeck and R. R. Hoffman. Hillsdale, NJ: Lawrence Erlbaum Associates. 3–24.

———. 1987. Proverbs, pragmatics, and the ecology of abstract categories. In *Cognition and symbolic structures: The psychology of metaphoric transformation,* edited by R. E. Haskell. Norwood, NJ: Ablex. 121–140.

Honeck, R. P. 1997. *Proverb in mind: The cognitive science of proverbial wit and wisdom.* Hillsdale, NJ: Lawrence Erlbaum Associates.

Honeck, R. P., and R. R. Hoffman, eds. 1980. *Cognition and figurative language.* Hillsdale, NJ: Lawrence Erlbaum Associates.

Humboldt, W. von. [1836] 1988. *On language: The diversity of human language-structure and its influence on the mental development of mankind.* Translated by P. Heath. Cambridge: Cambridge University Press.

Hume, D. [1749] 1902. *An enquiry concerning human understanding.* Oxford: Clarendon Press.

Hutcheon, L. 1995. *Irony's edge: The theory and politics of irony.* London: Routledge.

Hymes, D. 1971. *On communicative competence.* Philadelphia: University of Pennsylvania Press.

Inhelder, B., and J. Piaget. 1958. *The growth of logical thinking from childhood through adolescence*. New York: Basic.

Johnson, M. 1987. *The body in the mind: The bodily basis of meaning, imagination, and reason*. Chicago: University of Chicago Press.

Johnson-Laird, P. N. 1988. *The computer and the mind*. Cambridge: Harvard University Press.

Jones, R. 1982. *Physics as metaphor*. New York: New American Library.

Jung, C. G. 1921. *Psychological types*. New York: Harcourt.

———. 1956. *Analytical psychology*. New York: Meridian.

———. 1957. *The undiscovered self*. New York: Mentor.

———. 1965. *Memories, dreams, reflections*. New York: Vintage.

Kant, I. 1781. *Critique of pure reason*. Translated by N. Kemp Smith. New York: St. Martin's Press.

Kennedy, J. M. 1984. *Vision and metaphors*. Toronto: Toronto Semiotic Circle.

———. 1993. *Drawing and the blind: Pictures to touch*. New Haven, CT: Yale University Press.

———. 1999. Metaphor in pictures: Metonymy evokes classification. *International Journal of Applied Semiotics* 1: 83–98.

Kennedy, J. M., and R. Domander. 1986. Blind people depicting states and events in metaphoric line drawings. *Metaphor and Symbolic Activity* 1: 109–126.

Kinder, J. J. 1991. Up and down: Structure of a metaphor. In *Essays in honour of Keith Val Sinclair: An Australian collection of modern language studies*, edited by B. Merry. Townsville, Australia: James Cook University of North Queensland. 283–296.

Klein, W. 1994. *Time in language*. London: Routledge.

Koen, F. 1965. An intra-verbal explication of the nature of metaphor. *Journal of Verbal Learning and Verbal Behavior* 4: 129–133.

Konner, M. 1991. Human nature and culture: Biology and the residue of uniqueness. In *The boundaries of humanity*, edited by J. J. Sheehan and M. Sosna. Berkeley and Los Angeles: University of California Press. 103–124.

Kosslyn, S. M. 1983. *Ghosts in the mind's machine: Creating and using images in the brain*. New York: W. W. Norton.

Kövecses, Z. 1986. *Metaphors of anger, pride, and love: A lexical approach to the structure of concepts*. Amsterdam: John Benjamins.

———. 1988. *The language of love: The semantics of passion in conversational English*. London: Associated University Presses.

———. 1990. *Emotion concepts*. New York: Springer.

Lakoff, G. 1987. *Women, fire, and dangerous things: What categories reveal about the mind*. Chicago: University of Chicago Press.

Lakoff, G., and M. Johnson. 1980. *Metaphors we live by*. Chicago: Chicago University Press.

———. 1999. *Philosophy in flesh: The embodied mind and its challenge to Western thought*. New York: Basic.

Lakoff, G., and R. E. Nuñez. 2000. *Where mathematics comes from: How the embodied mind brings mathematics into being*. New York: Basic.

Langacker, R. W. 1987. *Foundations of cognitive grammar*. Stanford, CA: Stanford University Press.

———. 1990. *Concept, image, and symbol: The cognitive basis of grammar.* Berlin: Mouton de Gruyter.

———. 1999. *Grammar and conceptualization.* Berlin: Mouton de Gruyter.

Langer, S. K. 1948. *Philosophy in a new key.* New York: Mentor.

Lave, J. 1988. *Cognition in practice: Mind, mathematics, and culture in everyday life.* Cambridge: Cambridge University Press.

Lee, D. 2001. *Cognitive linguistics: An introduction.* Oxford: Oxford University Press.

Leezenberg, M. 1995. Giambattista Vico: Metaphor and the origin of language. In *Contexts of metaphor: Semantic and conceptual aspects of figurative language.* Amsterdam: Institute for Language, Logic, and Computation. 53–60.

———. 2001. *Contexts of metaphor.* Amsterdam: Elsevier.

Levin, S. R. 1988. *Metaphoric worlds.* New Haven, CT: Yale University Press.

Levine, R. 1997. *A geography of time: The temporal misadventures of a social psychologist, or how every culture keeps time just a little bit differently.* New York: Basic.

Lévi-Strauss, C. 1978. *Myth and meaning: Cracking the code of culture.* Toronto: University of Toronto Press.

Locke, J. [1690] 1975. *An essay concerning human understanding,* edited by by P. H. Nidditch. Oxford: Clarendon Press.

MacCormac, E. 1976. *Metaphor and myth in science and religion.* Durham, NC: Duke University Press.

MacWhinney, B. 2000. Connectionism and language learning. In *Usage models of language,* edited by M. Barlow and S. Kemmer. Stanford, CA: CSLI Publications. 121–150.

Malinowski, B. 1922. *Argonauts of the Western Pacific.* New York: Dutton.

———. 1923. The problem of meaning in primitive languages. In *The meaning of meaning,* edited by C. K. Ogden and I. A. Richards. New York: Harcourt, Brace, and World. 2–24.

———. 1929. *The sexual life of savages in North-Western Melanesia.* New York: Harcourt, Brace, and World.

Mallery, G. 1972. *Sign language among North American Indians compared with that among other peoples and deaf-mutes.* The Hague: Mouton.

Marks, L. E., R. J. Hammeal, and M. H. Bornstein, eds. 1987. *Perceiving similarity and comprehending metaphor.* Monographs of the Society for Research in Child Development Serial No. 215. Chicago: University of Chicago Press.

Marschark, M., A. Katz, and A. Paivio. 1983. Dimensions of metaphor. *Journal of Psycholinguistic Research* 12: 17–40.

McNeill, D. 1992. *Hand and mind: What gestures reveal about thought.* Chicago: University of Chicago Press.

Modica, G. 1988. Sulla fondazione del linguaggio in Giambattista Vico. In *Prospettive di storia della linguistica,* edited by L. Formigari and F. Lo Piparo. Rome: Edizioni Riuniti. 175–190.

Morris, D. 1969. *The human zoo.* London: Cape.

Neisser, U. 1967. *Cognitive psychology.* Englewood Cliffs, NJ: Prentice-Hall.

Neumann, J. von. 1958. *The computer and the brain.* New Haven, CT: Yale University Press.

Nietzsche, F. [1873] 1979. *Philosophy and truth: Selections from Nietzsche's notebooks of the early 1870s.* Translated and edited by Daniel Breazeale. Atlantic Heights, NJ: Humanities Press.

Noppen, J-P. van. 1985. *Metaphor: A bibliography of post-1970 publications*. Amsterdam: John Benjamins.

Noppen, J-P. van, and E. Hols. 1990. *Metaphor II: A classified bibliography of publications from 1985–1990*. Amsterdam: John Benjamins.

Nuyts, J. 2001. *Epistemic modality, language, and conceptualization: A cognitive-pragmatic perspective*. Amsterdam: John Benjamins.

Obler, L. K., and K. Gjerlow. 1999. *Language and the brain*. Cambridge: Cambridge University Press.

Ong, W. J. 1977. *Interfaces of the word: Studies in the evolution of consciousness and culture*. Ithaca, NY: Cornell University Press.

Ortony, A., ed. 1979. *Metaphor and thought*. Cambridge: Cambridge University Press.

Osgood, C. E., and G. E. Suci. 1953. Factor analysis of meaning. *Journal of Experimental Psychology* 49: 325–328.

Pagliaro, A. 1950. *Filosofia del linguaggio: La dottrina linguistica di G. B. Vico come chiave ermeneutica della storia del mondo*. Rome: Edizioni dell'Ateneo.

Palmer, G. B. 1996. *Toward a theory of cultural linguistics*. Austin: University of Texas Press.

Panther, K. U., and G. Radden, eds. 1999. *Metonymy in language and thought*. Amsterdam: John Benjamins.

Pavlov, I. 1902. *The work of the digestive glands*. London: Griffin.

Peirce, C. S. 1931–1958. *Collected papers of Charles Sanders Peirce*, Vols. 1–8, edited by C. Hartshorne and P. Weiss. Cambridge: Harvard University Press.

Penfield, W., and R. Rasmussen. 1950. *The cerebral cortex of man*. New York: Macmillan.

Penfield, W., and H. Roberts. 1959. *Speech and brain mechanisms*. Princeton, NJ: Princeton University Press.

Pennisi, A. 1988. Calcolo verso ingenium in Giambattista Vico: Per una filosofia politica della lingua. In *Prospettive di storia della linguistica*, edited by L. Formigari and F. Lo Piparo. Rome: Edizioni Riuniti. 191–207.

Perrine, L. 1971. Four forms of metaphor. *College English* 33: 125–138.

Piaget, J. 1923. *Le langage et la pensée chez l'enfant*. Neuchâtel, Switzerland: Delachaux et Niestlé.

———. 1936. *L'intelligence avant le langage*. Paris: Flammarion.

———. 1945. *La formation du symbole chez l'enfant*. Neuchâtel, Switzerland: Delachaux et Niestlé.

———. 1955. *The language and thought of the child*. Cleveland, OH: Meridian Books.

———. 1969. *The child's conception of the world*. Totowa, NJ: Littlefield, Adams, and Company.

Pinker, S. 1990. Language acquisition. In *Language: An invitation to cognitive science*, edited by D. N. Osherson and H. Lasnik. Cambridge: MIT Press. 191–241.

———. 1994. *The language instinct: How the mind creates language*. New York: William Morrow.

———. 1997. *How the mind works*. New York: Norton.

Pollio, H., and B. Burns. 1977. The anomaly of anomaly. *Journal of Psycholinguistic Research* 6: 247–260.

Pollio, H., and M. Smith. 1979. Sense and nonsense in thinking about anomaly and metaphor. *Bulletin of the Psychonomic Society* 13: 323–326.

Pollio, H., J. Barlow, H. Fine, and M. Pollio. 1977. *Psychology and the poetics of growth: Figurative language in psychology, psychotherapy, and education.* Hillsdale, NJ: Lawrence Erlbaum Associates.

Popper, K. 1972. *Objective knowledge: An evolutionary approach.* Oxford: Clarendon.

———. 1976. *The unending quest.* Glasgow, Scotland: Harper Collins.

Popper, K., and J. Eccles. 1977. *The self and the brain.* Berlin: Springer.

Reed, D. 1994. *Figures of thought: Mathematics and mathematical texts.* London: Routledge.

Richards, I. A. 1936. *The philosophy of rhetoric.* Oxford: Oxford University Press.

Rogers, L. 1998. *Wish I were: Felt pathways of the self.* Madison, WI: Atwood Publishing.

Rosch, E. 1973a. Natural categories. *Cognitive Psychology* 4: 328–350.

———. 1973b. On the internal structure of perceptual and semantic categories. In *Cognitive development and acquisition of language*, edited by T. E. Moore. New York: Academic Press. 111–144.

———. 1975a. Cognitive reference points. *Cognitive Psychology* 7: 532–547.

———. 1975b. Cognitive representations of semantic categories. *Journal of Experimental Psychology* 104: 192–233.

———. 1981. Prototype classification and logical classification: The two systems. In *New trends in cognitive representation: Challenges to Piaget's theory*, edited by E. Scholnick. Hillsdale, NJ: Lawrence Erlbaum Associates. 73–86.

Rosch, E., and C. Mervis. 1975. Family resemblances. *Cognitive Psychology* 7: 573–605.

Rucker, R. 1987. *Mind tools: The five levels of mathematical reality.* Boston: Houghton Mifflin.

Rumelhart, D. E., and J. L. McClelland, eds. 1986. *Parallel distributed processing.* Cambridge: MIT Press.

Russell, B., and A. N. Whitehead. 1913. *Principia mathematica.* Cambridge: Cambridge University Press.

Salem, L., F. Testard, and C. Salem. 1992. *The most beautiful mathematical formulas.* New York: John Wiley.

Sapir, E. 1921. *Language.* New York: Harcourt, Brace, and World.

Saussure, F. de. 1916. *Cours de linguistique générale.* Paris: Payot.

Schrift, A. D. 1990. *Nietzsche and the question of interpretation.* London: Routledge.

Searle, J. R. 1969. *Speech acts: An essay in the philosophy of language.* Cambridge: Cambridge University Press.

Sebeok, T. A., and M. Danesi. 2000. *The forms of meaning: Modeling systems theory and semiotics.* Berlin: Mouton de Gruyter.

Segalowitz, S. J. 1983. *Two sides of the brain: Brain lateralization explored.* Englewood Cliffs, NJ: Prentice-Hall.

Shannon, C. E. 1948. A mathematical theory of communication. *Bell Systems Technical Journal* 27: 379–423.

Shannon, C. E., and W. Weaver. 1949. *A mathematical theory of communication.* Chicago: University of Illinois Press.

Shibbles, W. 1971. *Metaphor: An annotated bibliography and history.* Whitewater, WI.: The Language Press.

Smith, E. E. 1988. Concepts and thought. In *The psychology of human thought*, edited by R. J. Steinberg and E. E. Smith. Cambridge: Cambridge University Press. 19–49.

Sontag, S. 1978. *Illness as metaphor.* New York: Farrar, Straus, and Giroux.

Sperber, D., and D. Wilson. 1986. *Relevance, communication, and cognition.* Cambridge: Harvard University Press.

Stachowiak, F., W. Huber, K. Poeck, and M. Kerschensteiner. 1977. Text comprehension in aphasia. *Brain and Language* 4: 177–195.

Staehlin, W. 1914. Zür Psychologie und Statistike der Metapherm. *Archiv für Gesamte Psychologie* 31: 299–425.

Sternberg, R. J. 1990. *Metaphors of mind: Conceptions of the nature of intelligence.* Cambridge: Cambridge University Press.

Stewart, I. 2001. Foreword to *1000 play thinks: Puzzles, paradoxes, illusions, and games*, by I. Moscovich. New York: Workman Publishing.

Swadesh, M. 1951. Diffusional cumulation and archaic residue as historical explanations. *Southwestern Journal of Anthropology* 7: 1–21.

———. 1959. Linguistics as an instrument of prehistory. *Southwestern Journal of Anthropology* 15: 20–35.

———. 1971. *The origins and diversification of language.* Chicago: Aldine-Atherton.

Sweetser, E. 1990. *From etymology to pragmatics: Metaphorical and cultural aspects of semantic structure.* Cambridge: Cambridge University Press.

Taylor, J. R. 1995. *Linguistic categorization: Prototypes in linguistic theory.* Oxford: Oxford University Press.

Thorndike, E. L. 1898. *Animal intelligence.* New York: Psychological Monographs.

Turing, A. 1936. On computable numbers with an application to the Entscheidungs problem. *Proceedings of the London Mathematical Society* 41: 230–265.

———. 1963. Computing machinery and intelligence. In *Computers and thought*, edited by E. A. Feigenbaum and J. Feldman. New York: McGraw-Hill. 123–134.

Tylor, E. B. 1871. *Primitive culture.* London: John Murray.

Ungerer, F., and H-J Schmid. 1996. *An introduction to cognitive linguistics.* Harlow, England: Longman.

Verene, D. P. 1981. *Vico's science of imagination.* Ithaca, NY: Cornell University Press.

Viberg, A. 1983. The verbs of perception: A typological study. *Linguistics* 21: 123–162.

Vygotsky, L. S. 1962. *Thought and language.* Cambridge: MIT Press.

Wapner, W., S. Hamby, and H. Gardner. 1981. The role of the right hemisphere in the apprehension of complex linguistic materials. *Brain and Language* 14: 15-33.

Way, E. C. 1991. *Knowledge representation and metaphor.* Dordrecht, Netherlands: Kluwer.

Weinstein, E. A. 1964. Affections of speech with lesions of the non-dominant hemisphere. *Research Publications of the Association for Research on Nervous and Mental Disorders* 42: 220–225.

Werner, H., and B. Kaplan. 1963. *Symbol formation: An organismic-developmental approach to the psychology of language and the expression of thought.* New York: John Wiley.

Wertheimer, M. 1923. Untersuchungen zur Lehre von der Gestalt, II. *Psychologische Forschungen* 4: 301–350.

Wescott, R. W. 1978. Visualizing vision. In *Visual learning, thinking, and communication*, edited by B. Rhandawa and W. Coffman. New York: Academic Press. 21–37.

———. 1980. *Sound and sense*. Lake Bluff, IL.: Jupiter Press.

Whorf, B. L. 1956. *Language, thought, and reality*, edited by J. B. Carroll. Cambridge: MIT Press.

Wiener, N. 1949. *Cybernetics, or control and communication in the animal and the machine*. Cambridge: MIT Press.

Wierzbicka, A. 1996. *Semantics: Primes and universals*. Oxford: Oxford University Press.

Winner, E. 1982. *Invented worlds: The psychology of the arts*. Cambridge: Harvard University Press.

———. 1988. *The point of words: Children's understanding of metaphor and irony*. Cambridge: Harvard University Press.

Winner, E., and H. Gardner. 1977. The comprehension of metaphor in brain-damaged patients. *Brain* 100: 717–729.

Wittgenstein, L. 1921. *Tractatus logico-philosophicus*. London: Routledge and Kegan Paul.

Wolff, P. 1963. *Breakthroughs in mathematics*. New York: Signet.

Wundt, W. 1901. *Sprachgeschichte und Sprachpsychologie*. Leipzig: Eugelmann.

Yu, N. 1998. *The contemporary theory of metaphor: A perspective from Chinese*. Amsterdam: John Benjamins.

INDEX

R

radiation, 87, 88
rationality, 56
reality, 86
recursiveness, 60
reflexivization, 78–80
relative productivity index, 92
rhetorical question, 24
Richards, I. A., 16–18
right hemisphere, 46, 47
Rogers, Linda, 101–02
Russell, Bertrand, 26
Rutherford, Ernst, 116

S

Sapir, Edward, 58, 64, 66. *See also* Sapir-Whorf hypothesis
Sapir-Whorf hypothesis, 58
Saussure, Ferdinand de, 65
science, 116–17
    scientific theory, 19
selfhood, 101
    the face and, 110
sensation, 29
Sense Implication Hypothesis, 39–41, 43, 44, 45, 55, 67
sensory source domains, 70–72
sentences, 62–64
    declarative, 62, 64
    diagramming, 62–63
serendipity, 121
series, 28
Shakespeare, William, 99
Shannon, Claude, 27
sign language, 115–16
simile, 24
Six Characters in Search of an Author, 123
Sontag, Susan, 25
Sophocles, 12
sound symbolism, 81–83, 98
source domain, 22
source domain hopping, 88, 93
source domain productivity, 93
Sphinx, 12
spirituality, 86
subordinate concept, 34–35
Summa Theologica, 14
superordinate concept, 34, 41
Swadesh, Morris, 82
Symbolism, 110–12
synecdoche, 24
Syntactic Structures, 60

T

Tagliacozzo, Giorgio, 5
target domain, 22
tenor. *See* topic
theater, 124
    origins of, 10–11
Thomas Aquinas, Saint, 14
Thrax, Dionysius, 64
time, 67–68
topic, 17, 18
transformational theory, 64
triangles, 35–36
tropes, 23–24. *See also* individual tropes
Turing, Alan, 27
Tylor, Edward B., 103

U

unconditioned response, 42
Universal Grammar theory, 44–45, 60

V

vehicle, 17, 18
verbs, 83
Vico, Giambattista, 5, 11, 14–15, 25–26, 32, 47, 48, 55–56, 83, 104, 107
    concept formation and, 41–42
    culture and, 85, 124–25
    spirituality and, 86. *See also New Science, New Vico Studies*
vision, 70–71
von Herder, Johann Gottfried, 66
von Neumann, John, 27
Vygotsky, Lev, 33, 34

W

Waiting for Godot, 123–24
Walpole, Horace, 121
Weinstein, E. A., 47
Wermicke's area, 45
Whitehead, Alfred North, 26–27
Whorf, Benjamin Lee, 58, 66. *See also* Sapir-Whorf hypothesis
Wiener, Norbert, 27
Winner, Ellen, 47
wisdom, 98
Wittgenstein, Ludwig, 81
Wundt, Wilhelm, 16

X

X-Bar theory, 61